winter of the salamander

winter of

harper & row, publishers
san francisco

cambridge london
hagerstown mexico city
philadelphia são paulo
new york 1817 sydney

the salamander

the keeper of importance

ray young bear

FIRST EDITION

Designed by Patricia Dunbar

Library of Congress Cataloging in Publication Data

Young Bear, Ray A.
    Winter of the salamander.

    I. Title.
PS3575.0865W5   1979   811'.5'4   79-4719
ISBN 0-06-452750-6
ISBN 0-06-452751-4 pbk.

---

80 81 82 83 84   10 9 8 7 6 5 4 3 2 1

This book is the tenth in Harper & Row's Native American Publishing Program. All profits from this program are used to support projects designed to aid the Native American People.

To those who helped me

A gwi ma i • na ta wi • a sa mi
ke ko • i i na tti mo ya nini • a yo
shes ki • ne ko qua ta be ya i ke

There are no elucidations or foresights
merely
experiments with words

contents

Acknowledgment is made to the following publications
in which many of the poems first appeared in one form or
another:
Pembroke Magazine, South Dakota Review,
Phoenix, Seneca Review, American Poetry
Review, Northwest Poetry Review, Cutbank,
Partisan Review, Dacotah Territory, Poetry Northwest,
Phantasm, The Great Circumpolar Bear Cult,
Anthologies: Come to Power, The Crossing Press,
            Carriers of the Dream Wheel, Harper & Row

Special thanks to the National Endowment for the Arts
for a grant which helped in the writing of this book.
                                        —R.Y.B.

1
because the
blue rain exists

grandmother

if i were to see
her shape from a mile away
i'd know so quickly
that it would be her.
the purple scarf
and the plastic
shopping bag.
if i felt
hands on my head
i'd know that those
were her hands
warm and damp
with the smell
of roots.
if i heard
a voice
coming from
a rock
i'd know
and her words
would flow inside me
like the light
of someone
stirring ashes
from a sleeping fire
at night.

painted visions

faraway trains ring the existence of time.
inside the cold end of a small rainbow
we stood like lonely eagles
huddled against each other,
wishing to ourselves a gentle warm stove,
images of our participation
within the human world.
all of us, standing in a cluttered room,
standing away from the sound of our talons
scraping the frost from the earth.

we turned to the people and mumbled
something about the little girl
who said she could hold her breath
forever and that she knew the very thoughts
of a blackbird with dreams of the day
it will skiprope on a sidewalk.

once those years of sharp rivers
took me to a place of caged bears
who sang an endless song to us about
the blank shield without our painted
visions.
wear what you are to us
through a safety pin over your heart.
the bitter knife will recede.

in the brilliance of summer:
the earth performs its life and death.
the house stands unpainted.
we stand on the bridge

made by the gods of the cold rock,
the cold underwater.

we regather a lost rainbow.
we walk somewhere near the lightning
and our hearts imagine themselves
as fire-burnt cottonwood trees.

to the north beyond the wall
of this room, a purple night-fire
burns in glory and our ignorance feeds it,
sustains it.

i grow back into a child.
i cannot name the people around me.
the differences in our life.
the things which keep us in circles.
broken pieces which once belonged
to us.

four songs of life

1)   a young man

the blue rain
quiet in feelings
losing
nothing—showing no one
that i am cold
in this earth
singing
different songs
i never heard
from the same people
unable
to create or remember
their own
songs to keep

2)   an old man

i sang
to the warm sun
and cold moon
this morning
and offered
myself
to the land
and gods
for them
to
teach
me

the old
hard tests of living
all over again

3)   this one

i remember well
my people's
songs.
i will not
reveal to anyone
that i know
these songs.
it was intended
for me
to keep
them
in secrecy
for they are now
mine to die with
me.

4)   the fourth

a time
in sadness
within the night
holding me
and comforting me.
here i am
being
taught
to be
a man
with life
and old sacred
songs to guide me alone
and love me
forever.

catching the distance

she closes her eyes for time
and the land, slender with meanings.

with the razor flicking above her arm,
she said, the blood will come out
through these holes. it will be
dark blood. its color will lift
as i inhale through this horn.

i went outside with my tooth
clutched inside my hand.
i thought to myself:
she will be well.
last night these skies
were filled with light
and it felt as if i was
just learning how to walk.
the earth seemed off-balance.
i followed a silver streaking star
until it exploded.
i felt comfortable
seeing the glint from my teeth
come back to me
before it rested to the north.

and from the bottom
of a kettle my grandmother
tipped over, small fiery sparks
representing a battle between humans somewhere,
raced back and forth. even after she had gone
into the house with the cooked food,
i was still kneeling over the black kettle.

i imagined some sparks coming out
and dragging away the dead.

i was called to eat.
my mother sat on the bed
with her bare back towards me.
the powdery medicine rolled itself
into the blood over her wounds.

there are plants breathing wisdom,
offered by earth, blooming on this land.
no one will give the time to learn.
i see myself as a snowy haze,
drifting slightly, turning around
always wanting to remember more.
sometimes it is clear and the wind
brings to my hand, many choices.

as a child, colored ribbons held me still
and smoke brought the day through
the longhouse. thunder and lightning
made some of us cringe under the tables.
years later, i stood under its black sky,
asking the creators of this world to forgive
my carelessness. i kept on dreaming night
after night that all i heard was the rumble.

the kettle still sways on fire
bringing my fears to a small comfort
for i can wait until this part of me
is over. i know there is a reason
to why tomorrow will come.
when it comes, there will be no need
to speak of parts.

the clouds threw this light

these horses were tainted and yellow
when dawn first brought the cold,
making my breathing like
an old man's, cautiously
coming through a blanket
soaked with tiny red suns.

last-night-rains came to
a black whisper, wove its tail,
and moved after my grandfathers,
still smoking the offer i gave
while they were here.

the clouds threw this light
into the horses and they were revived
by the rumbling in their bones.

i stand cradling my rifle, and
notice the day humming, swinging
my little sisters to sleep,
back and forth inside the old house.

doors

all they say he saw was
his younger brother's silhouette
trying to enter their sanctuary.
if it had been otherwise
people would have been permitted
to live endlessly.
for four days the younger
asked to be received
cried
he was alive and not evil.
the door never opened
to which he died and was taken
elsewhere.
it is wrong to speak out loud
of the older who did not accept the offer
for he is the one i say my life to. . . .

rushing

yellow november
comes swaying.
i feel the hooded man
drawing move on my friend's
back. in his brother
i see his face. black
pellets drop to the floor.
we had seen its flood.
the time we lied about
the stone and how it
was supposed to have hummed
away from his head.
his lungs are now full with
the rush of his bundled-
up life. bits of bread,
pie and cake are placed
in a dish. i smoke a
cigarette for him
and bury his clothes
on a hillside where
once a fox ran beside us.
his furry hands over his eyes.
i can still see the shovel.
the thought of a shotgun.
i heard that in the night
a deer whistled out his name
from a cornfield and gave
him its antlers spreading
his thoughts through
the passive quails.
years later, as i warmed
the shadow inside my coat

over the stove, my mother
announced she had found
a spring and she brought
the first taste to everyone
who was there. in some mornings
as icy as it was, i washed my face
in it, sometimes thinking
of the hooded man and the fox,
the rushing sounds of a river
under our house.

these horses came

1.

from inside the bird a dream hums itself out and turns
into a layer of wind rushing over my face that needs
a small feather from the badger's nose to blow away
and create corners where i will stand and think
myself into hard ways.

2.

these horses came on light grey clouds
and carried off the barbed wire fence-post.
i am thinking about a divided bird
divided into four equal pieces.
the snow falls over the thoughts of each man.
in their stomachs the winter begins.

3.

the railroad tracks steal a distance
and the crows fly off chipping memory
from their wings. in my eye there are words
and i am reminded of a story i once fell
asleep to.

i aim my rifle at the sun and ask:
are you really afraid of children?

mix these eyes

whenever it came that close
i never sheltered myself
from the sad
moving with the woman-horses
recalling those grassy hills
where sometimes
a day or night would lose
tiny wet children
and then taking
whatever appeared as a feeling
to a nearby stream and drinking
their reflections to forget
the spin inside old soft eyes
the constant sorrow of her mind
of grown sons and growing grandchildren

the wooden casings of three
curled tip philippine knives

when your eyes turn down
i go back
remembering how often
the number of days
my arms folded to the table
and my head how it disengaged
from me decided to close the doors
from long days

whenever it came that close
the bundled hair and the braided corn
came talking in unison
one time of the two brothers
who held the sun on its crossing
how one cried after
he witnessed a fish-spear slice
through an eyeball

i wish i was the air under the ice
children sleep on the floor
we can hear the whistling
of their wooden ribs

we knew the badgers and the foxes
were something more: they stood
on the other side carving the trees
into simple wooden bowls filled with hearts
divided as bear   thunder   eagle   fox   fish
and wolf
before we appeared fitting ourselves
into them

between his fingers

selected women and their children
went over the hills to pick
berries to be consumed sacredly.

i sat inhaling the smoky protection
coming through the ground
rather than the coarse wood.

yellow horses waited discerningly
against the oncoming day
speaking of the stillness
which followed their decisions
and ours.

he took a knife, cast it to the air
and said: seek a tree
from it whittle a stick
find this *one* and make a hole
between all his fingers
drive the sharpened stick
its length and then bring it
back and tell me if the corn
he has planted will grow
to be used.

the river stood behind the sun
and passed to the sun a small speckle.
the sun took this gift
and soon understood its meaning.
in respect, the sun combed his hair
but in the morning
he opened his bag where

16

he kept things that were given to him.
things he did not trust.

it was windy that day and spider webs
were in the air offering rides to the river.

war walking near

death designs swirl high above faces that are of disbelief.
a captured people dressed in red hold hands and hum
to themselves a strange song.
brown rain slips fast into a sad freedom
low in the thoughts of the old man
who visioned the coming revolution.

he tells to his reflection a small word
not to reveal that in the night
he controls the night enemy
night-enemy-who-takes-us-with-magic-medicine.
he heard the eagle with eyes of war walking near.
they say the spring air comes without much intention.

seeing at night

say these are the ones seeing only at night.

if the standing place emanates cold
enemy sent wings flap peculiarity
from tree to tree and behind will sway
the old woman covered into a shawl.

i woke early morning and it was dark then.
i went outside looked at the swirling
restless forest.
she arrived with her small kettle.

the little people on the hillside
again have not showed themselves to us.
i guess the prayers along with the tobacco
were heard and absorbed the time
they wandered near our homes.
no one seems to know if it's
the good or bad which travels
with them.

ahead, sudden sickness in our children
will make us inquire.

they are targets accepting food readily
from acquaintances really the ones
whom we should fear.
the medicine men of the north
have all the right answers.
they know how to stop spells.

i feel the beginning catching up
and so i must stop
and go.

one chip of human bone

one chip of human bone

it is almost fitting
to die on the railroad tracks.

i can easily understand
how they felt on their long
staggered walks back

grinning to the stars.

there is something about
trains, drinking, and being
an indian with nothing to lose.

morning-water train woman

it didn't take much talk for her
to realize that her brother
was drunk
a couple of years ago
when the morning wind blew a train
into his sleep
spreading the muscles and fibers
of his body over the tracks
prematurely towards the sun
claiming another
after the long stillness of bells
now jingling with persistence in her ears.
maybe we convinced her
in accordance to time and place
about this life where we walk with but few friends,
feeling around for reception
at our presence
willing to exchange old familiar connections
with no forgiveness added to our partings.
perhaps she is still thinking of new methods
by which to end herself
this coming weekend or the next.
surely it won't be the same
as the last time she tried:
taking a bottle of aspirins
and downing them with a can of engine oil.
the people just laughed and said:
there are other ways, besides. . . .

one time before she went away
i dreamt of her
sitting on the tracks

attentive to the distant changing colors
of the signal post.
i knew what she thought and felt.
there were images of small black trains
circling around her teeth.
their wheels were throwing sparks
setting fire to her long stringy hair.
her eyes withdrew farther back inside
the skull of her head
afraid of the scars,
moving and shifting
across her ribs
like long silvery railroad tracks.

the sun and the morning

we stood that day peeling potatoes
for an old woman
and spoke too often of skimming visions—
as easily as opening your eyes
and asking for permission to walk
through the rain with your little bucket
to catch it in—
because you thought you had heard it
soaking into the window
and making strange tapping noises
as it came closer
after it had circled the house four times.

i mentioned my feelings
for trains
which reminded me of small whirlwinds
spinning across the backs
of old white crows
flying the night without instructions from their masters.
you said exactly.
i knew your fingers
rubbed the tracks eight times
spitting out your words
with bits of coughed-up blood to make things easier,
and hurrying the long way home
making sure that your trailing-shawl is not touched
by the sun's fingers
whose daylight can infect you with black rotting skin.
though both of us try to live everything
the hard way,
there was one
who tore out his heart so that the children
would live slenderly without troubles.
it will become harder
when you try looking for us
for we blend too quickly with each other.
maybe sometimes shoulder to shoulder
like two crows
who sit on the sand
with our bellies full with the found meat
sharpening our talons against the rocks
and then
flying back to the old and hungry ones
our beaks drying in the wind and sun
the crust unable to come off
when we wash our faces by the river.

oasis

i often saw you with towels wrapped
around your head,
hanging over your eyes rubbed
with the shadow of woman's oasis smile.
at dusk, carlights always gave you
away at your usual place:
walking the ditches.
my mother said you cooked each meal
for your mother laid in bed unable
to stand, looking out the window
till night.
did you ever think about the white
arabian horses that i buried
by the stream?

birds with tears in their bones

the dwarf slept until the birds banged
against his eyelids,
but it was only after great effort
that they succeeded in opening
his hollow eyes.
their opposites flew out, black, ruffled,
and fierce,
needing the water from the cold
springs.
to them it meant life for their master
and a hope of reviving him well enough to walk.
he had been asleep all through winter,
trying to figure out the old ways
by which he once practiced his medicine.
he did exactly as he was told:
he camouflaged himself in the berry bushes
and he aligned his pierced fingers
to the three positions of the moon.
he achieved his partial invisibility
and he caught crows as they danced on skulls
with their bellies full with the horsemeat,
and he listened to them,
smelled the enemy-lightning in their breath
as they mumbled and cackled about the different ways
they held counsel in trees,
the effectiveness of the unborn horse
inside the womb,
how they killed themselves as they grew old
by asking gentle words to come down
as a hail of ice—
it was honor to bleed along the rainbows.
days climbed inside his head,

filling it with secret upon secret,
and smiling whenever his straw-like reed
penetrated the hearts of humans.

one night, as he flew about checking
upon the images of himself,
standing around the points of his home,
he caught a green light glowing in the pine-trees.
he released it after it had changed into a firefly
and he followed it hovering across the paths.
it circled houses he often watched.
after following it over several hills,
he began to realize that the firefly
was aware of his intentions.
the firefly stepped out from the shadows
and greeted and announced himself.
the dwarf felt cold beads of water forming
on his wings. when he blinked his eyes
he expected to see a person, but before him
stood a one-legged salamander
speaking in a slow and leisure way that it was he,
the spirit of the salamander who spread
news of death. the salamander pointed
to him and he saw his house on fire.

no magic he had compared to that of his.
he thought of his children and of the moments
he gambled with their lives.
the salamander told him to forget his magic.
the dwarf stood crying and pleading
as the salamander hobbled away.
he promised him but he knew it wouldn't work.
the seasons came and he absorbed the powers
of all those who knew no prayers to anyone.
he stayed away from puzzling funerals.
spells and dreams returned.
he remembered the last time he woke.
he saw himself on the beaks of small birds.
the birds cherished his bones and he would sing

of salamander faces, flat stones,
magical voices, and the frozen ice
over the river.

parts: my grandfathers
walked speaking 1970

white buffalo runs sleeping through snow and mixes
me into animal bones avoiding to be struck by daylight.

red colored evenings accepted the meat
thrown as offering over this man's old sky shoulders.
it seemed that while he skinned his kill
songs were composed from the difficult life
of earthmaker and he sat with a knife
eager for his wind
to carry body scent other directions.

there are in a house of many years
my shoulders held by fingers of the sun.
a mourning woman who sat in the continual middle
arrived in disguise as mother and wrapped a red
                                        blanket
over my ways and edges even after
i had explained to her that i had known
of her before and that i knew of her intentions
of splitting the day and night in half
                              before my eyes

of sending the man with horns
with the body of a horse
walking and dancing into our paralyzed dreams.

she combed my hair with the wings of the seeking owl
properly
in the forests away from the houses.
she sang of spring birds and how brown running
                                        waters
would signal to the appointees to begin
family deaths by witchcraft.
she showed me a handful of ribs.
i leaned too close to the sun and felt the warmth
of peyote brushing and pumping its images
into my blood and heart
                        of a birchtree
giving birth to crystal snowflakes.
i washed my face with the water from the thunder.
i listened to the reasoning of two crows
who had chased spirits away from men who had
fasted for fourteen days.
i thought of an intended life and autumn came shyly
bearing songs but no gentle children.

woman of the horses sat in my circles.
she created fire burning only on the occasion
when boars cleaned the skin of people
from their teeth beside green rivers.
the northern lights carried the meaning
of being far past the sufferings of night enemies.
old men inside rainbows offered no messages
but whispered of another existence closer
to a prayer than tears.

my grandfathers walked speaking in choices
across the black sky.
i stood inside them and released my hand
which held my words gathered into parts
of the earth.

signs

the winter must be here.
everyone grows weary
as they change worlds
not knowing which to learn
or which to keep from.

my grandmother wears
her sweater even before
the day is halfway through.

she is thinking of snow
and the times she will brush
it off the green rock.
the hungry dogs and how unaware
they will be.

the fire will eat the food
in memory and for the strength
of her grandchildren.

i rub my face against the window
feeling the change will
never take the place for me
feeling everything i am
it will never be enough.

like a coiled wire

i am sitting in a hallway
ahead of me i feel the sound
of my legs brushing against
each other through the stiff
new pants

like a coiled wire i am walking
through friends and relatives

we each had to tell each other
that we didn't belong
to be far away from home
away from the idea of what
we should be

in this hallway i woke up
into a fog wearing brightly
colored clothes and i found myself
again

even then i couldn't believe
the presence of mountains

and when after three days
had gone into my life
i decided to walk
to the mountains

i kept walking over and coming
upon hills and rows and rows
of houses

and the white rocks on their roofs
finally made me realize that the mountains
were too far

i thought to myself
they're going to take it
away from me as well

trying to fill the empty
spaces in my mind
i became the train i rode on
passengers without direction

racing through dark tunnels
gently in between and out of sleep
my body convinced we are home
because of the way the birds
sing and that echo

two times

two times i've seen
the great water and where
the land comes to an end,
where the standing spot
bends to the sky,
where the bird's wings
shaped the last cliff.
two times i remember
seeing and touching stones
on the sand beside the rotting
flesh of seals.

two times i stood apart
from the shell gatherer
and unwrapped from the green cloth,
from its tiny leather knots,
my offering to the water door
of the man who rode
the spiderweb.

two times, my grandmother's
white hair. two times,
the grey waves of the ocean
brought the muskrat
and the newly found earth
together.

poem for viet nam

i will always miss the feeling
of friday on my mind.
the umbrella somewhere
in the dumps of south
viet nam. in exchange
for candy it will hide
the helicopter.
franco must be here
in a guy's heart. i've
heard so much about him.
the closest i got was when
i machine-gunned
the people waist deep
inside the brown speckled
swamp. the castle where we drank
the sweet wine from giant fish bowls
has come against us. we knew that
when we killed them they tasted
the blood of whoever stood
beside them. some of us
thought of our families.
the cactus warms in our
bodies. the old mansion
where his friend played
cards has murdered his
brother and we see the stabbing
right through the door. while
i ran i made a song from
my wind. i have not held
this god beside me. only
this rock that i've often
heard about stays and at times

feel it must be true. his words
are like my dreams. they are eating
balls of rice in front of us.
i heard them talking a couple
of yards ahead of us. the jets flew
in v formation and they reminded me
of the wild ducks back home. once,
when i looked down, my wrists opened
and i wiped the blood on a tree.
i can only sit there and imagine.
they were ear close. the next day
i wore their severed fingers
on my belt. my little brother
and i hunted while someone close
was being buried on the same hill
where we will end. we hardly knew him,
coming into his family twelve years
too late. it was a time when
strawberries came bearing
no actual meanings. the bright
color of our young clothes walks
out from the fog. a house speaks
through the mouth and mind
of the silversmith. we saw the red
sand on his boots. what do we
remember of him? i remember he
said good-bye that one fall.
it was on a sunday. he was slender.
the burns from a rifle barrel spotted
half his face. april black is somewhere.
i scratched his back knowing
of sacrifices. the children
growing up drunk.

wooden men

the day is now here
she said
if you feel the cold wind
in your face
please know it's for you
to allow the need for
explanation
wooden men
of earth
that we are
cannot be mistaken
what it took to live out
our selection in
pointing at you

i dream of teeth moving along
the clear side of a fog
carving notches into sticks
my lungs regret the inhale
of smoke and ashes
smudged faces and misconceptions

for the spring
to will itself to produce
us good weather
it must be demanding
several tornadoes
touch the ground
and houses splinter
rapidly into
a thousand pieces
dead people tumble

in the air
amid the debris
of their personal
effects

i have tried hard
not to change
because i know
what it has meant
to me
how i
as a dark green river
has changed its course
i open my hands and
bits of sand slide
through my fingers

coming back home

somewhere inside me
there is a memory
of my grandfathers stalking
and catching robins
in the night of early
spring for food.
the snow continues
to gather children
outside, and i think,
as long as they are moving.
the frost sets itself
on the window before
the old man's eye.
we sit together
and imagine designs
which will eventually
vanish when the room
and talk become warm.
he goes over the people
one by one and stops at one,
because he can't find any
answers as to why she took
the instrument and used it as if
she were one. they do not like
her much, he says, dancing barefoot
with tight clothes, taking the songs
into a small black machine.
it's how you breathe and space the song.
the same old crowd will be out
of jail soon, and then,
back again. the trees
will be running with sweetwater

and hard work is to be expected.
there is much error in the way
we carry our being and purpose.
we covered everything with his
conclusions and sometimes
he balanced his confusion
with a small gesture and said,
better to leave things like that
alone. nobody will understand.
i pressed my fingers
against the window, leaving
five clear answers of the day
before it left, barking
down the road.

santa ana winds

i hear the ocean water
swishing inside my ears.
the winds continue to grow
hot. ash comes down off
the burning mountains.

sleeping all day,
nobody ever came to wake me
among milky answers.

i left a trail of spit
on a sidewalk untouched.

she has children
crowded in her kitchen.
by handfuls she stuffs
indian corn into their
grimy mouths.
like lovers we go to her,
determined.

everything would
without failure
end up in my room.
my brother would be there
sighing immaturely:
son of a bitch.

disheartened,
i agreed.
autumn.
ducks.
corn clicking
in their stomachs.

to remember the smallest

listen to the words coming
from our elders when they mention
our blood drying inside us and how
it peels
shedding itself
the more we pretend
with each other
the way our legs tire easily
and how they collapse
as if by purpose when
in flight from legless
crawling spirits
who notice that we do not wear
turtle feet around our necks
their fangs are set to bite us
the intent being to release and extract
lies we have fed to our bodies
a minor part of life nobody needs
is the reply i hear
i try to make your eyes
blend farther inside mine
to make you see where
we stand distant from
our actual places
holding on to our phantom arms
the only comfort we feel
i ask for your name when
the feeling comes to tell you
of this but you are constantly absent
or else you reason that it's of
little value besides being late
i sometimes *speak* for you

and i think you do the same
because i have seen it in your face
when i talk about my veins and how
i have tied them to the dawn
and how i hang suspended
above the earth
refusing to eat away my veins
as you have done

morning talking mother

tonight, i encircle myself to a star
and my love for the earth shimmers
like schools of small rainbow-colored fish,
lighting the drowned walnut trees inside
the brown flooded rivers
swelling birth along the woods.
i think of each passing day when time expands,
bringing the land against my chest
and the birds keep walking as they
sing wildly over our house:
be in this daylight with me.
push yourself from the walls.
let me see you walk beneath me.
let me see your head sway.
let me see you breathe.
everyone has been up into the daylight.

i walk over her head and remember
of being told that no knives
or sharp objects must pierce
inside her hair.
this is her hair.
another grandmother whose hair
i am combing.
there are paths winding over her face
and every step is the same:
the feeling of one who is well known,
one who knows the warmth rising
as morning talking mother.

in her hands she prepares snow for the visitor.
she sprinkles the snow into the bare hills
and valleys where in the spring
after the plants have grown
people with medicine eyes come
to lift the plants from her head
taking them home to the sick.

i remember as i was looking out
from my eyes that my eyes were like windows
smeared and bent out of proportion,
that the earth was curved from where
i was sitting. cars came and disappeared.
it was summer and i sat on a blanket.
i watched my grandmother as she came to me,
holding a skillet. she set it down beside me
and she fanned the smoke which came from medicine
crackling over the hot coals
towards me.

usage

she said
the plants
were in
shape of
birds,
moving around
at night,
could be heard
at times.
i never asked how
they were
used.

trains made of stone

until that sun or that circling spark
which keeps asking for an answer agrees to
either keep still or leave me alone,
i will sleep without pain,
without condonation.
looking outside, there are prints
in the snow, but no one thinks
the snow can walk. we are him.
a final moment breathes and we are mixed
securely into the winter months.
the choice has been here,
waiting for my decisions,
whether i will allow myself
to turn old, spinning hazily
through stories just once more
to feel like a keeper of importance,
ignorant of the leaves changing color,
ignorant of where i stand.

there are two light-complexioned sisters
camouflaged with ash and grey cloth,
watching the roads on sundays,
hoping to catch a glimpse of my body
drag itself over the warm purple stones
on the railroad crossing.
i listen to the sleet.
i know which color best represents
the day, why the heron sights us
even before we round the river bend.

i can't be like the ones before me.
i can't make my mother see.

i know of her feelings
as well as the past.
i believe in this walk towards
the west after death, but that's only for some
who have suffered and prayed through their lives,
preparing.
three times i was the slender bird praying
beside a well near dawn. these clouds drifting off
were the doors of my friends.

the old woman was an owl
of death. she approached my mother
at the gathering and whispered that
one of her daughters would have trouble
living.
my little sister danced as a part of day,
leading the others slowly towards a time
when all things would be reversed.
i was away when news of her will to dance
carried inside, telling me that the river
will never swell and give birth to lies.
i have found life this way and i will leave
like one, knowing that it has not passed.

the otter swims on to others

it is still here, the four-day-old rain
cold with the vow of belief,
a need to see a certain glint from the sun,
a desire to smell the scent the seasons share,
an extension of the bright yellow buffalo,
floating and stopping over each wooded hill.

its light spreads to the sleeping children.
they nervously twitch to the sound of thunder.
the thunder who made these children.
and the hummingbird whizzing through the day
stops at the day's end beside a tall flower,
wondering what part he plays to the children,
to their guardians. if anyone will ever
use him as an instrument to both heal
and destroy.

nothing with human meat and sinewy legs runs
informing others of news.

out in the middle of a river,
there is an island and it was there
where i felt akin to the otter.
i stay away from him, but i eat the food
he brings me. i'm not anybody anybody's looking for.
i'm the person who came and appreciated
the worthless too late.

the otter swims on to others.

i look down and see the river rise
over my body. there are too many tests to pass.

i know well ahead that i'll fail this one and i know
of the man who will blame me for it. the others who
follow him, listen to him. without anything to
follow, my life is on this island.

once, overwhelmed by the feeling in the air,
i sensed inside the longhouse the turning of sky
and earth. clouds and hummingbirds to remind me
of my loss. i heard above the weeping
and the singing, the humming voice of a woman.

i breathed in her presence hoping to become
all in one instant all that is desired in a human.
from my lips i sent my loose words:

grant me any existence. pass me for others.
take the unborn child and let it be him
whose name will be remembered when the frozen
lake is chopped open. let someone protect
the coming seasons. remind whoever it is not
to be taken in so quickly.
not to be the fools we have been.

2
when we assume life will go well for us

four poems

my reflection
seems upside-down

even when the daylight pushes
my shadow into
the ground

it is like that

      *

this little house swallows
her prayer
through the green fire
and stone

i disappear
into the body of a mouse
sleeping over the warm
ashes

     *

i am walking and i
notice that the road
seems bare

some of the stones
are missing

ahead is a toad
throwing stones
from his fingers

whatever thought
he is following
we are
following

     *

through the cracks
along the walls of this
house

the sun reaches its peak

our dishes begin
to breathe

the crow children
walk my circles in the snow

the buffalo breathed quietly inside
past visions of winter
as he thought of one time
when he stood on some far hill
with a shiny red blanket on his back
warmed by a bird who blew rain
into his eyes and saw
old white wolves lying on their thin bellies
gathered into a circle and eating the ground

that bled as if it had been torn
from an enemy's shoulder during battle
or a child's heart
suddenly coughed up without reason
but the times then
were hard and too real to be accepted
like a grandmother asking you
to comb her hair in the daylight
and you know she wants to tell you
what she saw and felt:
there has been someone floating around here
last night
carrying a small bundled bag
pierced by long sharp bones.
it has waited long enough
grows afraid and wants to take another person.
again it has sent a green fire through
our small land
freezing ears and anything
within its glow stands still.
for only through this way
it can be sure of not stopping
on its travel somewhere
and seeing its shadow on the morning ground
with the sun ripping its face apart
and dividing the skin to the eager crows:
the crows crying like women
when they find themselves talking to each other
in their master's voice
their children throwing up small green pieces
of warm flesh
and looking confused when their throats
suddenly leap out at the thought of white wings.

the woman's vision

from a row of trees
i see her face.
she carefully examines
the bulges on her stomach.
she is a snake in search
of its den, of a man looking
for stories in the wood.
there is a glassy twin
of himself and around him
are clouds of his frozen
breath, drifting, and we
meet them on the road.
there is a baby in a cradle
designed with beads,
brown and yellow ribbons,
spotted symbols for stars.
she remembers the twin
and the man reappears,
carving the image of her baby
into a tree, heating his knife
over a fire, burning in the figures
of black, ruffled, birds,
turtles, to be sure the trees
fell down.

the way the birds sat

even for the wind there was no room.
the wind kept the cool to itself
and it seemed that his skin
also grew more selfish to feelings
for he was like a window
jealous of the light going through
denied his shadow the sun's warmth
when being alone brought him
the cool.

the way the bird sat
dividing the weather through songs
cleaning the snow and rain
from the underside of its wings
was evidence.
in its singing the bird counted
and acknowledged the changes
in the coolness of the wind.
he somehow held the bird responsible
as it flew about taking in puffs
of air. often the image of blue
hearts in the form of deer
crossed his mind outdoing
all magic and distortion
of the hummingbird who had
previously been the source
of his dreams. the bird
who had tunneled through
the daylight creating lines
in the air for his people
to follow.

his thoughts took him out
into a cornfield where he found himself
bundled up into a blanket thinking about
deer. the hummingbird
who had been dodging the all-day
rain stopped and hovered beside
him before it intermittently began
drinking water from the leaves around.

having killed and eaten so many deer
it was wrong to blame his weakness
on the sun and wind.
to accuse anyone nearby he thought
was as foolish as the consideration
to once save his morning's spit
with the intention of showing it
to people as proof that his blood
and time were almost out.
he even wanted to ask
if it was possible to leave it behind
for worship but all this faded away
like the flutter of wings
he always heard shooting past
the shadow of his foot before it
touched the ground.

once his nose bled all day
and he saved the blood
in his kitchen cups
testing himself to see if
his notions were true.
he emptied them in the yard
and just before the sun left
the standing cup-shaped forms
glistened.
when he woke the next morning
he couldn't find one.
he looked everywhere.
on the grass
under the porch

until he thought the whole event
a prescience.

the daylight was full and the birds
walked through his yard
speaking to each other
and sometimes gathering
around the area where he had set
his blood.

it was strange as he watched.
each time they walked away
from the area it was smooth
and intentional.
in his mind it reminded him
of a ceremony and he left lines
on where each bird had stepped
where each had circled
what words it might have said
even the prayers it might have sung
and when the birds had sticks
in their mouths he saw the singers
with their notched sticks.
their beaks moved up and down
the sticks made a rasping noise
and when the women hummed
it was a song he knew very well.
he danced to the rhythm
as the weather forced him
to watch from the windows
of his house. most of the birds
had the faces of people he had met
and lost. there was one he couldn't
recognize. although it was getting
dark he could tell that one wore
the face of a deer. he was still
puzzled long after the downpour.

the cook

with the thinking of winter
no longer enclosing her
to her room, the combing
woman with the mirror smiled
as she idly watched the lard can
swing from the cook shed.
the kettle chains would soon
be unwrapped from the newspapers
and it refreshed her to know
she would soon be asked to
cook for praying families,
to laugh among the other
women.

the image in the mirror
worried her. it folded
her face carefully into
the sides of the apron.
here was the other person:
the one who knew exactly
what she felt and thought.
the person in the mirror told her
it was there for a purpose
and that was to double
her knowledge of roots,
hanging them on strings
from wall to wall in her
house, arranging them
by the power of their use.

when it was time to flow
the mirror knew first and it

showed her by fogging up
the windows of her house.
the birds with their breath
would then come, drawing
pictures, feeding her clothes
to the fire.

she felt the birds were
disappointed in being what
they were, always walking
up the trees, counting holes
endlessly, shining the sun
off their stomachs onto her
hands. she would caress her hands
over her face and every time
she did this, the rain would come
out from the fields, breaking
the winter and spring apart.
as the weather divided, the birds
would watch the combing woman's
lips and it reminded them of their
own shadows, three dwarfs
in search of tobacco,
wooden faces of death.

the seal

in the corner of this
old woman's house,
sits another, of the same
age unable to speak
but able only to grunt
and moan like a seal,
doing a yes or a no
or a strange maybe.

people say when she
was inside her mother's
stomach, her mother
went to a circus, but
some also say it was while
swimming that she brushed
her body against a seal.
in time, the misfortune
is still here.

the winter's heart

the winter's heart has been placed
into a small delicate bundle.
a young boy who first discovered it
underneath a blanket of snow explained
that it wandered aimlessly, that in
exchange for warmth and the attention
of a weedless squash garden, it would
promise to the clan a longer life than
others.

so it is here, beside the nocturnal fire,
moving about and taking in breaths of air,
instructing, but with it came a human,
half-buried, hidden in the forest.
on occasion the clan elders were
to have conferred with him,
but like thoughts from us
as we walk in step
passing each form and object,
he was quickly forgotten.

this is what happened.
they are no longer religious drunks
and the human in the forest has since
transformed into a mineral.

in dream: the privacy of sequence

always expecting the winter
to be a sad one
i slept after heavy eating of food
and waited until the portions
grew alive.
they sprouted antlers and formed
into circles,
fitted themselves perfectly
into my hollow teeth
and communicated to each other
about the comfort and quiet welcome
they were to receive:
of imitating the distance
between the sky, earth,
and the children
shaping a figure from the snow,
recognized and visible
in the eyes of old people
quickly running to their trunks
and fires,
unpacking the contracted faces
of relatives, arguing who
was born the closest to the dead:
long trails of smoke streamed out
from the houses that rested
deep inside the hills.
trees stood about with their arms
stretched out over their foreheads
blocking out the sun,
wondering why the children's
laughter covered everything
in the whole valley including

sound. the trees turned to
the old man who had been sitting
in front of the sun.
the old man right away thought
he knew the reason why the trees'
eyes closed when he met them
with his. repositioning himself,
he pretended to gaze out past
them. he knew they had lost
the question. relieved, he
whistled like a bird and then
realized much more the quietness
that was in the air. without birds
or leaves or anything to travel
in the wind with except his
acknowledgment which went from
tree to tree being refused
at each ear. feeling strange,
he stood up and saw for the first
time, children running in the open.
the multi-colored kites in their hands.
the old man was familiar
with the various faces in
the sky and once in his dream
the kites came as disguised gods,
needing the lives of children
to prolong theirs.
it is just like flying a flag,
running away from a fox, going
back through the hole you
crawled through.

outside, the depicted visitor
standing in place of the weather
gathers himself around me,
holding in each hand, two
branches, strings of dried hearts,
the coming hardship of death.
with a mouthful of ashes,
he digs into the earth

hoping to save his warmth
for the otter who sleeps without
dreams, or without me to stand
above him, reminding him
of the cold, the dark thin birds,
the memory of their consumption tied in
little bags.

forgetting the good
of the coming spring,
my fingernails grew long
like brittle shovels
and dug out the squirrel
and pheasant from my teeth,
thick and warm, resembling
rocks.
i thought of the forest
where the deer killed people.
i had seen this one man's body
lying beside a fence which
bordered this forest. it looked
as if they had poked after
the bullet with their fingers
tracing the clot. farther
down i saw the man's head
propped up against a tree.

i found myself between the airs
of changing weather
unable to distinguish what
to kill, layers of wind over my eyes,
growing old and uncertain,
skinning and cutting out
the kneeling children from
the bodies of animals.
i throw the food to my dog
who refuses to eat although
he knows it is a worship to his skill
and lets the others crowd in.
once, a boy with puffed-up

eyes took out the roof
of his mouth and sharpened
his knife on his heart.
smiling, he licked the knife's edge
and proceeded to carve for me
a boat with arms and legs.
all night, the boat
struggled to lift its burnt
belly to the stars. sensing
that the boy had fallen asleep,
daylight came, took the boy's
knife and sliced off the boy's
fingers, crushed them,
dried and sifted them with
its hands and breath until
they changed into trees.
the particles that blew away
from the daylight's breath
made the boy dream that
he had rubbed his hands
against the sky.

her husband

despite irregular occurrences
and the sudden accumulation
of her years, she was content
to be inside her humid, small
framed house.
it alarmed her that she had
unknowingly removed her sweater.
a rare gesture.
stacked under the table
her canned goods looked as if
it would be a tiring job in
deciding which one would be
best to open and to eat.
the flies with their buzzing
wings made the place loud.
there was a peculiar sensation
in her throat indicating she had
succumbed to a fever
and whatever collected in
her lungs also attracted
the flies.
in the middle of summer,
she thought, today, a day
to have soup without crackers.

she had lived in the land all
her life and had seen her husband
some of her children die as she held
vigil beside their beds, unable
to revive them but pleased
their suffering was short.
she often wondered if anything

mattered to her, if she had
adhered to her spiritual
walk.

in her walks she found herself
in doubt and always headed toward
familiar roads to places where she
once grew.
these were barren places.
the trees which were there
in bloom and the skeletal huts
where she cooked in seclusion
were the things which remained.
the chickadee's stuttering call.

another face

small eyes water on the branch
they have been there
for a long time now
thinking:
please move your wings
to show me i have found you
at last.

*   *   *

this rock halfway out of the snow
turns away from the daylight
and cradles small blue footprints
into its stomach.
at night, they mark the snow again
keeping close to the rock.

waiting to be fed

she swam smiling in the river
thinking it was good that she
had come out here to be with the sun
going out into the air
and giving warmth to her sisters' faces
watching her from the sides
listening carefully for the hum
of human voices.
no one would show up here today
she thought. it was too hot
to swim with the sun
radiating on the wings of insects
flying in repetition
between shadow and sunlight
confused in their decisions
evident by the sound
of their open mouths everywhere.

through the years to now
she had known the river well.
sometimes she imagined herself
a rock under the water
surrounded by a landscape
that would bend the trees
through the sky
and then through the stars
reminding her of burnt holes
in cloth that protected
her hand from fire
while cooking for people
waiting to be fed.
she knew a place where

it was like this
where it suddenly became cool
and clear. this place
had often been mentioned
in her mother's constant warnings
about rivers.
like the insects and the sunlight
she released her thought
to a spiderweb drifting
across the river
breaking through the clouds
losing all revenge to the giants
lifting their heads in their watch
to her swimming over the cool
gushing spring
coming up from under the river
thinking of her stomach
and how it was growing fast.
the child swimming inside her:
the touching and speaking of two hearts
made her feel she could smell the sweetness
of the baby's skin in her breath.

in time she would be able to see
the face inside her stomach.
a dream indented on her body.
she took care of it
as if it were a god
as if the snow in winter
had already begun to take shape
in the hands of children
far from the staring foreheads
of their houses.
she knew it wasn't sacred
but everything in the land
seemed that way.
everyone took great interest
and care for her that she
could somehow make out visible
strips of gentleness gathering

around her body
streaming out from her family
a circle of suns.

she looked at her reflection
floating over the water.
it seemed as if the sound
of water was also the sound
of rustling leaves.
her sisters broke her thoughts
when they suddenly stopped
talking. she quickly asked
if there was anything wrong
but they remained motionless.
from a distance she could
not tell if they were playing.
it was a long time before
she found herself shouting
and hitting at the water
hoping they would start
moving. soon her sisters' hands
indicated a discussion.
she could not hear their words.
she felt her body drifting
away taken by the foam.
the water rippled to the banks.
seals crawled out from holes
she hadn't noticed before.
she could feel the cold
water as the seals swam by
brushing the bodies of her
sisters against her stomach.

she felt twisted in a dream.
there was talk around her
and she could sense by the words
being spoken that it was night
and that relatives were inside
the house being fed. each one
chewing and then

quietly nodding.
her mother's hand covered her head.
there was whisper from the root
telling her to be still.
she died as she gave birth.
the child lived without ever hearing
or speaking.
she lived in the shadows
of her keeper's house
and was taken care of all her life.
sometimes she would go out into
the daylight and rock her body
back and forth as she sat
on the porch.
a smile on her face.
her arms and legs folded to her body.
the sun deep inside her eyes
walking to the river.

spearfishermen

the sun has melted the ice
over the river
down the middle
from the north
and south

it stops where
the men are filling
their bags
with frozen
fish

most of them
are grinning
every now and then
they burst out praises
to whoever
speared
the largest catfish

no one can believe
the spectacle
of all the fish
swimming
under the river
in cycles

unwanted fish
swim in packs
above dark shadows
of prehistoric
fish

men peer into
the water and complain
about the dull reflection
the silver coffee cans
are making

they curse seeing
the two bright spots
on the tail of the fish
disappear
in the corner
of their eyes

the sun has reduced
the ice into a single
narrow bridge
over the river

most of the men keep
to the side of the river
they're on
but there are a few
with courage who cross
from side to the side

trying to exhaust
all possibilities
of finding even bigger fish

the others patiently
watch their holes in the ice
occasionally they see
the spots
and every time
it's too late

the strain of the arm
muscles seems foolish
the prongs
from the spear

dig deep into
the sand

and every time it does
it is an ugly sound

star blanket

the cracks on the walls
of the summer house
divide the earth into pieces
of blue knots on a string.

we are in night
as it is outside.
sightless, i grow
into my patients,
arrange them in the order
of their warmth.

the sound of a bird.
its wings.
the flexing of my bones
makes the beans shake
by the woman's feet.
a single leg begins to move,
gets up and fits itself
over the cracks.

i see whistles
catching and eating
the gourds as they spin
and talk on the dirt
floor, nudging everyone away
from their boundaries.

with my fingers together,
a man loops leather
around them, tying them
to his. inside the star
blanket, i hear the wind slapping
the canvas over the roof.

the intensity of light
is felt and everyone grows
concerned, appoints
the door-faced man
to climb to the roof,
covering the night
more securely.

at my feet,
a row of sitting men
are level like trees.
i hear their wings,
sounding hollow,
filled with conversation,
boring a hole in the sky.
the smell of wood
everywhere.

swallowing a small copper
tube, i light up the people's
bodies and detect malignant clots
traveling freely like worms.

the tube brings back
the sickness while i grind
the red rock with my teeth

74

into sand, mixing it into
the grey and blue holes
of the woman's inner skin,
patching her bag of busting
water.

as the tube goes out
again, i feel the mouth
of a baby attaching itself
to the tube,
gesturing to me,
depressed with the one name
it has.

i fit my heart on one end
and breathe out of the copper
his name: two men lying
to the third.

the place of 1

i'm not without you.
it's such a warm day
to wake up to,
to still feel yourself
dreaming,
always ending up where
the dead wake unexpectedly
with the mourners
taking it naturally
until the one dead
loosens his blankets
and walks around,
sorts you out from the rest,
tells you it's no longer
important and sends you on
to another dream of less importance.
the relatives hold up their faces
to the day with smiles and false
attention to the children.
they'd like to have the day
go quick. there's hardly
any time to gather our thoughts.
my grandmother sensed that you
had walked by, stopping and entering
her house for a drink of water.
she heard you place the dipper
back into the pail.
announcing your absence,
my uncle breathes hard.
i picture the walls of the house
breathing. heat rises from the stones
on the road. all morning you had been there.

the sun warming your back.
your fingers touching the earth
for the last time. the girl who was
with you still looks at the hole
in her thigh. bits of grass and mud.
it still isn't over. i was up most
of the night, taking myself apart,
rearranging my head, thinking how beautiful
it would be to lie beside your cousin,
to have some people or passersby standing
around us. the gun between us. the sound
of a car coming down the road.
blood glistening between the cracks
of our grey mouths.

the place of m

a short day has grown
into the sky,
balancing itself
between our places
of breathing.
the thought of warm
roomlight has left me.
the thought of our
hands against the house,
measuring each corner
and each window
has left me.
the snow melts on
the ground and the yellow
of corn appears in the eyes
of flying birds.
the food you left
for the wandering man
walks behind you.
the killer's car
sits under the sun.
its eyes skim over
the walls of the house
looking for signs that
will make it remember
but it doesn't find
anything except a boy
carrying a boy who keeps
on fainting, falling
into seizures.
from the fog, an old man
troubles his weak legs

to kick the stones alive.
his moist face attracts
you, tells you to leave
the past alone.
you offer the comfort
of your finger to fit
around his finger like
a ring so that he may glance
at it every now and then
now that he is walking away in his
father's hands in the form of five
sticks.

celebration

the little girl dressed
in purple,
a pattern of sealed eyes,
comes to the foot
of our bed,
signals her presence
and runs away from us,
dropping from her fingers,
a handkerchief filled
with well-chewed peyote,
fifteen cups of steaming tea,
wet circles in the wood
on the floor,
the name of the man who

chewed the peyote into
a ball.

outside, i see
through the frost
on the grass,
a snake,
coughing out hundreds
of babies in her dream
of falling,
dreaming of the young boy
who takes half of the green
roundness in his mouth,
hides the other half
on the bone of his wrist,
inhales the smoke from
burning sheaves of corn.

the snake is a woman,
her hair the sound
of horses,
an arm walking over
the soft white spots
of a frozen river.
she breaks through the ice
and two hearts float
to the surface.
each bearing her mouth
and my nose.
it was easy being made
to exist and to not breathe.

men with wings
of smoked birds,
porcupine heads,
dance under the plains sun,
under the lights
of mingling medicines.
the people in their dancing
pause to hear the laughing

of drunks, the other
drums along the ridges.

at home, away from
the celebration,
a girl inserts herself
with a clothes hanger,
smears her guilt on the windows
thinking of the deaths
of her half-brothers.

decorated children walk
away from campfires.
the cowboy-hatted singers
grow weary under the shade
of damp pine branches,
gather their heads
to the middle,
talk among themselves
about a trick song,
two deaths in one day,
and the girl whose
parents rushed home,
scraping the insides
of their daughter off
the walls, bending
the wire hanger back
into shape and taking
care of it as if it were
a child.

this house

i begin with the hills
lying outside the walls
of this house.
the snow and the houses
in the snow begin somewhere.
the dogs curled against each
other must feel they own
the houses, the people
in each house must feel
they own the dogs
but the snow is by itself
piling itself over everything.

i keep thinking of comfort
such as a badger stretched over
a house with its guts pulled
out. its legs over each corner.
it is truly a dream to tie down
a skinned badger like a tent over
a house, watching it shift
as the wind changes direction,
like the cylinders of pistols,
the holes of magnums turning
people inside out.

my young wife turns under
the yellow blanket in her sleep.
she wishes to be left alone,
closes herself within the dark
of her stomach, cups her hands
and sees what is ahead of us.
she senses i will die long before

the two of them, leaving her
without a house, without roomlight.

the yellow blanket, the house
and its people cover her.
the clothes she wears cover her.
the skin of her body covers her.
the bones cover her womb.
the badger feels it owns the womb,
protects the unborn child,
encircles itself to a star
and dies in our place.

in missing

the stars in your perpetual face
reflect on the window
and they glow on through
to yesterday, floating past
the illusion of gathered boars.
the prints of my hand
on each boar collect
the snow as it delicately
drops from the sky.
i want to think the trees
are hearing me think.
i haven't seen my brother
for a long time. i keep

thinking that his time is spent
watching the air move between
the river and the ice.

there are small faces with
cupped ears looking for
tobacco. from the north
a man comes to us and wraps
himself in a blanket.
he tells us he represents
the starry night. he covers
his whole body except his legs.
his helper goes over the blanket
with a rope. we are asked to remove
our glass eyes.

even with the blanket
i remember his fingers were
entwined with blue material
and white ribbons.
he kept saying to us:
i am the wall of these coughing
sticks. i have flown down to
the woman who believes there
are children packed somewhere
in her belly. we've brushed
our wings up against her,
but she keeps insisting
that she must point at her
younger sister. there is a tree
with strings of beads all around
it. a girl cried and then we sat
still.

i imagined a white bird
imitating the old man's voice.
he could see its face. the suddenness
of her daughter's miscarriage. i feel
lost. somewhere i remember my grandmother
leading me up a hill. we came to a tree

and she pointed down at the ground.
we stood for awhile before we each
touched it.

from his dream

the air hadn't changed
since she last saw her mother.
the land was covered with frozen
rain. she knew a couple of days
ahead that the spring would disappear.
she kept reminding to her husband,
it'll have to come back.
i don't think it's really over with,
but he always seemed disinterested.
a look of worry in his eyes.
even as it was snowing,
thunder rolled across the roof
of their home and they couldn't
help glancing at each other
with puzzled faces. bodies
of disemboweled animals flashed
in their minds,
the children ran about in play
but when they ran into their father's
eyes, they could see the light
of their rooms, the changing contrast
of shadows, clothes that had to be buried,

faces of death, a knife burning in
the figure of seals on a tree.
the second time they ran,
the wind made sounds as if
there were people with their mouths
up against the house, talking.
as it grew colder, the snow made
more noise against the plastic
coverings over the windows.
when the children looked outside
they could see the clouds piling up
on top of each other, each group
darker than the other.
across the room where their mother
sat they could distinctly visualize
the changing color of her lips.
teeth biting into her skin.
they followed as she circled
the room, spitting the chewed willow
all around the windows.

their son had been gone most
of the day. it wasn't unusual for him
to hunt alone. he always seemed to know
what to do. old enough to be gifted
naturally to keep away from flowing women,
he had spoken about sliding down hills
on his knees, picking up the snow
to his ears and hearing the thoughts
of deer, bringing packed bodies
of muskrat and duck, the different
crusts of blood on his shoulder bag.

from a distance, his father
could see his tracks heading
into the thickets. small owls guided
their way through brush by the touch
in their wings. he remembered a dream
he had that morning of giant fish
and coral snakes submerged in the icy waters

of a river he had never seen.
he and his son cornering a small horse
covered with fish scales, bearing
the head of a frightened man.
its thin legs and cracked hooves.
somewhere in this land he knew
there was a place where these creatures
existed. he had also been told of a hole
where the spirits spent their days,
watching the people before they crawled
out, traveling through their arcs
in the sky towards evening like birds.
on the way back home, thinking his son
had circled the forest, he crawled
across a section of river which was still
covered with ice and fish entrails,
previous spots where he had taught
his son to use a blanket to block
out the daylight to lie there
with his barbed spear, waiting
for catfish to lumber out from the roots
of fallen trees under the ice.
although he felt a desire to crawl
straight across without looking
down into the river bottom through
the clear ice, something caught his eye,
and as he peered into the bubbling water,
he saw the severed head of his son,
the hoof from his dream,
bouncing along the sandy bottom.

the last dream

the old man was already well ahead
of the spring, singing the songs
of his clan as well as others,
trying to memorize each segment
and each ritual, the differences
of the first-born, who would drink
the water from the drum, why it
was hard teaching the two-legged
figurine to connect itself
to the daylight, wondering
which syllable connected his body
to that of a hummingbird's
to have its eyes and speed,
why it was essential to be able
to see and avoid the aura
of hiding women. their huts
were visible along the hills,
draining the snow of its water,
making the winters visit much
shorter, but deep inside he knew
he had no regrets. the way
the bird sat, the way it cleaned
its wings, the way it breathed
told him he had kept his distance.
the winter had been friendly.
with only one dream to think
about, he collected the cold bodies
of muskrats given to him
by well-wishers and proceeded
to cut open their bellies,
carve their bodies into boats,
and positioned their bellies

to the sky, hoping for snow.
it was easy every time his
food ran out to hobble over
to the road knowing he'd get
a ride into town for groceries
and back, making little use
of his cane. it wasn't unusual
for him to look out his window
and see families bringing him
whiskey, bright-colored
blankets, assorted towels,
canned triangles of ham.
his trunks were full
of the people's gratitude.
through the summer and fall,
he named babies, led clan
feasts, and he never refused whenever
families asked him to speak
to the charred mouths of young
bodies that had died drunk.
he was always puzzled to see
their life seeping through
the bandages, the fresh oil
of their long hair,
the distorted and confused
shadows struggling to catch up
to their deaths. he spoke
to suicides just as he would
to anyone who had died peacefully.
he knew it was wrong to ask them
to go on, but he couldn't refuse
lives that were already lost.
everybody counted on him.
each knew that if they died
within his time, he would
be the one to hand them
their last dream,
the grandfather of all
dream.

winter of the salamander

i've waited through my wife's eyes
in time of death. although we have peeled
the masks of summer away from our faces
we have each seen the badger encircle itself
to a star, knowing that a covenant with his spirit
is always too much to ask for.

unlike us, her birth-companions have gone before us,
resembling small jittery waterbugs who keep
bumping into each other, unable to perceive
the differences between the eyes of their
children, the light-colored seals
camouflaged with native tongue
and beaded outfits.

we'd like to understand why we breathe
the same air, why the dead grow
in number, the role i play in speaking
to mouths that darken blue with swollen
gunpowder burns, chapped lips, and alcohol.
we keep wondering whether or not we'll ever
leave in the form of eight sticks.
we have waited until morning to turn off
the lights, hoping to catch a glimpse
of light chasing light.

there was a man whose name was k.
there was another whose name was m.
they knew they shared the same father.
the car of their killer sits within
the fresh snow. their grandfather sits
within the thought of a hummingbird,

women arriving at his request,
the mistake in the deaths of his grandsons,
the spell that came back.

they say: the mixbloods know of one
chance to be a people.
some of us, knowing of little dispute
in our past, forget and we assume life
will go well for us, life after death
being automatic. they are told
to absorb themselves into religion,
to learn and to outdo some drunken
fullblood's life. and me: like a dim star
i shine on and off in the midst of many
who have sat repeatedly within this line
of seated men, singing into the ears of leaves,
fresh twigs of the fresh green bean.

alfred and pete are still godless.
the morning has shown itself through
the windows of their houses, dissolving
the peyote in their stomachs, mixing
into the meal of sweetened meat and coffee,
half-man, half-horse, the green shirt
and the lamb.

turning eagle and i sit in the roomlight
of the salamander's two houses.
within the third house the windows frost.
at the beginning and end of each winter
we sit here before a body the size of our hand.
we made ourselves believe that no one
was responsible. we took the sound it made
from its last breath and we imagined a dwarf
hanging from the rafters with a lighted
cigarette in his mouth, reminding us
of the midpoint in the day.

the black kettle in the corner changes
into my young wife and she walks over

to the road with a small dish of food
and kneels down into the ditch,
whispering her mother's name: i invite you
to share with us this food.

3
in the brilliance
of the summer
daylight

in the first place of my life

in the first place of my life
something which comes before all others
there is the sacred and holylike
recurring memory of an old teethless
bushy white-haired man
gesturing with his wrinkled hands
and squinty eyes for me to walk to him
sitting on the edge of his wooden
summer bed

being supported and guided along
like a newborn spotted fawn
who rises to the cool and minty wind
i kept looking at his yellow
and cracked fingernails
they moved back and forth against the stove
and they shined against the kerosene-
                           darkened
kitchen and bedroom walls

i floated over the floor towards him
and he smiled as he lifted me up to the
                           cardboard
ceiling and on there were symbols i later read
as that of emily
her scratched-in name alongside the face
of a lonely softball player

remembrance two: it was shortly after he
                           held me
or else it was a day
or a couple of months

or a couple of years later when i saw him next
the bodies of three young men leaned against him
as he staggered out towards the night

i never knew what closed him
why i never saw him again
he was on the floor with a blanket
over his still and quiet body
above me there was a mouth moving
it was the face of a woman who had opened
the door for the three young men
she pointed to his body
this is your grandfather

and then i remember the daylight
with the bald-headed man in overalls
he too mentioned the absence
of my grandfather
i understood them both

i picture the appletree and its shade
as he was talking to me i saw a group
of people on the green grass
on the ground were table and linen cloths
with bowls and dishes of fruits and meats

the bald-headed man in overalls stood
in the brilliance of the summer daylight
his eyebrows made his face look concerned
or worried

later he stood on the same grass
he had been chosen to fill my grandfather's
empty place

the new colored blankets around his waist
and chest glistened with the fresh
fibrous wool
the beads reflected the good weather
the earth and its people stood and danced

with the beautifully clothed man
who was my grandfather
standing in between time
watching the daylight pass through
his eyes

from then on i only saw him occasionally
he would stand on his tractor
waving to each passing car on the road
as he drove home from
the soybean fields
or else he would converse with my two uncles
that the blood which ran through their
                                        father's veins
and theirs was unlike the rest of the tribe
in that it came from the beginnings
unlike ours

a woman's name

the faces who grew up
with me are still here.
i can only ask them
and they'll tell you
i haven't done wrong.
the huts of my seclusion
have all gone.
i've wrapped the cooking
chains in newspaper
ready to be given away.
through all of this,
the trees stand for a purpose.
they remind me of the time
i lived here, walking around
with my heart, my horse,
singing to anything
but afraid to meet anyone
who might catch me
with my mouth wide open,
the sun inside,
warming the bandaged
body of my child,
lost for good.

before leaving me, the poem: eagle butte and black river falls

for glen eagle speaker, alfred driver,
la force bearbow, oran and wesley wolfblack,
whose songs come to us in the form
of small plastic boxes,
it can't be easy composing through alcohol
and vision, constantly thinking
of the newly released album,
each of them miles apart
from each other,
common lives and interests,
going over what they collectively
remember of that day they chose to sing
and record:
the food, the pepsi, or the coors
they might have had.
any organic substance that might
have coated their delicate and holy throats,
feeling the fibers restrain them,
depressed with hangovers and witchcraft,
learning the lesson of the man
with the voice of four men
all over again.

each of them would like to see
our faces, to see whether or not
we honor and respect their voices,
their years of dedication.
hot, dry summers. the many faces and styles
of various tribes, the famed fancy dancers
and their costumes of cowbells and porcupine.
the prestige which befalls any young girl
who by the end of summer discovers herself

pregnant, sitting through winter,
beading his outfits and listening to him
boast about his capabilities,
his bustles, feathers blessed with sacred
incense. the drums and their p.a. systems,
whirls of dust and medicine,
mingling floodlights of power,
scattered tents and new trucks,
drunken families.

aside from their songs, we learn
from the jacket covers of their albums
and by word, the names of their drums:
eagle whistle, ashland, rocky boy,
mandaree, and, thunderchild
of saskatchewan.

the day settles into the dark green
horizon of spring. the cool wind that comes
through our windows relaxes us.
we are lost within our minds,
within the new grass dance songs.
lying here, husband and wife,
in the thick smoke of cigarette.
each of us reaching over to the tape recorder,
turning up the volume of our supposed history,
a 90-minute memorex.

the loud and pulsating music draws
the white students to their windows
and they stand quiet behind the curtains,
listening to the intense sounds
coming from their neighbors' mobile home,
the indians. larry, the white man,
puts his arms around to the front part
of kathy's swollen fish belly,
spreading his fingers over the imagined aura
of creation and flesh,
forgetting his curiosity

of tribal past, mixtures of blood,
limitations.

far away from their shiftless breath,
farther away from the sweetness
of the baby's breath in kathy's breath,
there comes a song through the window
about a poor, drunken man in the rain
whispering the words of his gods,
riding across the earth with their horses,
demonstrating to the humans the importance
of seals, of men just as gifted as him,
singing at celebrations,
"it is only for you. we have no place
in this song. within this daylight,
dance for us this song we are singing
for you."

strengthened by the season's new songs,
my wife and i took my grandmother
to black river falls, wisconsin
unsure as to whether or not it'd
be a worthwhile trip, unsure of my driving.
sometimes seeing ourselves in a nightmare
of blood transfusions on the highway,
the metamorphosis of our bodies
into sticks. on the outskirts of la crosse
we drove into a valley of stone cliffs.
this would be the closest we would ever
come to mountains. i was overtaken
by the abrupt beauty of the land.
a selected place in time,
harboring the powers of the mystical
and the lonely, gods and dwarfs
peering down from the hills into our car,
fixing the memory of our faces
into their minds. the secret blessing
which guided our way to the northeast
memorial day weekend.

when we arrived the celebration
was just starting. people from all tribes
stood numbed by their tents and concession stands,
looking far into the celebration with greed
and jealousy, wearing their chokers
and turquoise, anything to help
some give the impression of being
indian. some of the people we thought
we knew walked by as if we had spoiled
their fantasies and right away we felt lost
and disoriented. we kept staring at each other
when most of the motels rejected us.
over hamburgers and coke, my grandmother
spoke, "some people try to hide their lives
as long as they can, but we see them
and help them when members of their family
pass away. it doesn't work to feel important."
somehow i knew it was the same for me.
i was no better, but for a moment
it came in the form of a small whirlwind,
rushing in my dream in search of pinetrees,
waiting for me to be uplifted and shaken
from the fog; to find myself within the cracks
of the whispering walls, undergoing test
upon test, wondering whether or not
we'd ever be together like this again.
the three of us, pressed on by the people
around us to go our own distorted ways.

the spider: a naked body
in the summer

it would again come as if nothing
had happened.

i would enter it in my writings
as something whose force i had already
envisioned,
something we each lose and gain.

these walls are familiar
and then the next thing i'll say
is, i guess i have really
forgotten how it feels
to be on the other side
to have the burden
of a summer shadow.

i have seen a house of my own.
there is a station wagon
and we are inside

and i am waking up in you.
you hold my cubist drawing
above you.

did you do this?
it's pretty good.

if we have sex our hangovers
will go away.

only for awhile, kid.

i like the sensation that i am
having of remembering.
the light sprinkle of rain
stops above the pinetrees.
you kept talking about
your younger sister.
we can't do this.
i can still see the pain
in her eyes that night we saw each
other at the softball game.

i sat on the steps of the house
and everyone who drove by stopped
and expressed how much they felt
sorry for me, how stupid i was
to begin with, anyway.

you know, i have always imagined it.
somehow i knew last july
in the one moment when i was singing
in thought about how i would one day
drift back.

i wish i could get angry.
i did my best to invite the invisible.
in my mind i see chunks of apples
and burning cigarettes.
please stay away from the twin sisters
who are in heat.

all day i have seen you

it would have to be a very good reason.
i would see you off and then the next thing
i'd know you'd be gone, permanently.
everything that is us is represented
by the secondhand furniture.
i keep thinking i can withstand it.
it's easy to sit towards the east
on a summer evening, erasing the memory
of your absence with a cold beer.
all thoughts centered on the birds' airway.
the small dish of food which i placed
by the stream last summer was the closest
and only thing i did to remind the dead
and the sacred of my presence.

once, a one-eyed rabbit came right up
to me and i greeted it. another time,
a ground squirrel ate its way through
the plastic garbage bag. it dragged out
a photograph of us holding each other.
both of our eyes lost in miscarriage.

it would have to happen on a dull grey day
like this. i like to make myself believe
that i will have things planned long before
you have notions of leaving me.

you walk towards me from the west
with your head bowed down. the sound
of a bicycle leaves behind you. all day
i have seen you hanging clothes.
as you walk towards me you lose your

footing and i catch you by your wrist.
i ask how you see me. i always thought
you were kind. you know that one boy who
everybody thinks is a pervert? he's going
to wait for me until i finish school.

a tall and lone figure comes out
from the house and we hide behind
the station wagon, swatting mosquitoes
with the one towel which i eventually
give to you. i don't trust him. he is
good friends with the *fly* now
in sioux city.
how do you see me?

july twenty-six/1975

what could i have done if i had
been there? i grew tired of sitting.
the trees are there.
i can see the baseball diamond.
the power of one word of need
and coincidence.

it's hard to perceive sisters
beating one another senseless
with belt buckles, but i can see
the dents on the hood
of this car.

i need this trip.
i can't attach my thoughts
to anything specific.
we're going to be away from
everybody and we're free to do
as we choose.
again, the spacing in our lives
has shifted.

i open the glove compartment
and i discover a strange postcard
of an eagle landing on a cliff.
i tilt it and it repeats
the same sequence.
eight frames.

mounds of land race by.
i sense the long bronze body
of the car enjoying itself,

asleep and relaxed,
traveling over the stone
smooth highways
of eastern nebraska.

my cousin looks at herself
in the mirror and carefully licks
the taste of chicken
from her lips.

her son, the crow, talks
noisily to our grandmother
about the one day when they will go
back to montana to look for his
father, the reservation pig.

i think to myself,
what's the purpose of thinking?
i can't get rid of what has
happened. it's a shame that
i have dragged these people
into a troubled summer.

the brush in the land grows
more heavy and green.
we pass a carload of indians
headed towards the opposite
direction. macy.

we took the wrong route somewhere.
i don't know who's to blame.
i'm still pondering about
last night.

i see the approaching sign.
winnebago indian reservation.
my grandmother points to an old
deserted house in a ditch.
she tells of the time
when as a young girl she slept

there via an attempted rape
attack.

we are here on the second day
of this tribal celebration.
i fold my arms and head
against the steering wheel.
i've got to write a letter.
i drink a cup of warm milk.

dusty cars and staring faces
combined with the hot sun
hurt my eyes.

i start the letter:
this is from walthill.

the characters of our addiction

i am a long ways off from where
i'd like to be. days like today,
i dream which is the reason
why we are presently here.
my error.

there is a farm. i shoulder
a high-powered rifle.
through the binoculars
i see the two headlights.

three of my uncles are seated
around a polished table.
they are cheerful and they
enjoy the food.
we pretend things have returned
to being normal.

i selected this place.
i wanted to have a forest
nearby.
puzzles collapse in order.

all i want to do is to write.
something. the lawn mower speaks
for everyone. to the majority
of whites on this block,
it represents the spring.

one of the landlords just came
and asked why the electric company
couldn't get in to take a meter

reading. i replied, the door
is usually locked.
we'll make arrangements.

all right.
he takes one last piercing look
into the kitchen and living room.
as he walks towards the door
i pull a pistol up to his neck.

i picture myself in the desert
clutching my stomach with my fingers.
the stars are green plants.
my feet turn to incandescent hooves.
i take a bite out of the antler's
green bitter face.

we all share the last cigarette.
we untie the primal ropes from each other.
my wife places the bacon
between the paper towels.

a woman who has tried the duration
of her life to abstain
from the bad
falls into the corner of a house.
her eyes are crossed and foam
comes from her mouth.

her husband, the alcoholic,
picks the lint from his sweater.
my wife accepts a box of clothes.
it seems like there's always
a daughter returning
or else there's a baby
half-obsidian, half-clay
going from family to family
a short-loved novelty.

the furniture shines
with the day. i keep returning
to the land in my thoughts.
a shadow will refuse my offer
of wine and when it comes
into whichever house i am in,
we will not draw silence.

i sit here in abjection
all night. nothing planned.
towards morning i am still
singing long after
the station wagon
passed by, having seen
rochelle in oklahoma.
long after a different car
had passed, carrying the memories
of a film on bloodied oceans,
the time spent after being
forgotten.

we are a puzzle.
for one night, the parts
are mixed. the characters
of our addiction are elsewhere.
i feel a person sitting
on a porch. i am to someone
a voice, a sound.
we breathe each other's breath.

memories for no one

i feel the oven warm itself
next to me. the electricity
hums all through the walls
of this apartment.
we are entangled in pipes,
miles of moving water.
my wife is in the living room
beading rosettes.
the television is in perpetual
conversation with itself.
i look at my silver
wrist watch. it's about time
to put the pizza in.
excuse me.

seems like nobody really
appreciates the coming spring.
it's going to be hard for everyone.
nobody knows what's going to happen.
people tire from each other's company.
seek new faces and times.
i like to think that i'm not like that.

ten more minutes.
outside, the campus bells
make music. students strain
their minds and bodies walking by
deep in eyebrow thought.
the fastidious moon hangs in the mist.
he will make memories for no one.

it is morning and i have just
closed the windows. the birds
crowd on the branch and they signal
each other. all of them sing directly
into the one window that's open,
simultaneously.
my wife is still beading.
the television voices remind me
of the way people speak when death
is present. it's soft and you can barely
hear anything but you know it's
important.

i see a figure of a man running
towards the door of our house.
i motion to him that i can't open the door
because of the layered ice. he approaches
and i see the deceased face of my son
fully grown.

on the wall there is a picture
of flowers and on the second night,
rain is falling.
nothing matters anymore.

i am like a naked spider
in the summer, feeding from
the rain, imitating the fresh sprouts
of plants.

the moon and the stars,
the stone and the fire

i take my pants and shirt off.
my father and brother survey the area
towards the house before undressing.
it seems right for the summer wind
to feel good. i listen to my friends talk
under the clothesline.
heat from the fire warms
my legs. my mother speaks:
the stones are not enough now.
she digs them out from the red ashes
and rolls them into the canvas hut.
she each gives us a towel and for no reason
i inspect it, following the hemmed edges
with my moist fingers. the moon
and the stars give us extra light.
i look at my mother as she hastily
rolls up the sides of the hut.
i have spent the middle of my summer
without my other *self*. i hope when i enter
she will feel how much i miss her.
is it right to feel this way?
i go through the opening in the hut.
i sit and cross my legs, making room
for my father and brother who i can see
settling into their places.
i hear a voice resounding from
the shadow of my father praying
for the essence of the stone to cleanse
us of the ill will around us, to cleanse
our bodies of any physical illness.
i see my brother russell hunched over.

he needs all the power which will come
into us. i don't want his food to come
spilling out every time he has eaten.

they ask for recognition

within our lives
there is an impossibility
but as i am shifting from day
to night in your absence i am convinced
it is only one-sided.
it's regrettable:
the surroundings an eagle has,
eluding man, me,
a perennial tunnel in the sky.

i would prefer to turn back and look
where the stars and waves from the river
combine.
the triangle of our hearts.
the canvas which shuts us from
the universe.
we are complex.
there is an immense hate
that you have to be attentive
to what is being opened for you
whether it's candy or a can
of beer.

stay away from people
who can't stay in their places.
we see the time in their stomachs.
the clocks they have swallowed.
daughters and sons appear
and they ask for recognition
from sets of different mothers.
outside, we are not in compliance
to our divisions.

it's not the same.
did i actually know people?
this is only a river of clear blood.
no matter how many lies we record,
we still pack and congregate like flies.
we utilize simple and ambiguous words
to get by. we are accustomed
to the dream of our voice being wound
around a small, notched stick
buried under the fall's foliage.
it has a song of jealousy,
disparity,
the sound of two illiterate sisters
in flight.

in the weeks ahead i grew thin.
today i bow my head,
explain to myself:
spirits of houses and unseen children
equal a father and his sons.
i observe my voice being dug up
from the past.
on a certain spot along the ridge
on this hill there is a hole
in the ground where it once held
smoldering ashes, a smooth, ageless
rock.

in disgust and in response to indian-type poetry written by whites published in a mag which keeps rejecting me

you know we'd like to be there
standing beside our grandfathers
being ourselves
without the frailty
and insignificance of the worlds
we suffer and balance
on top of now
unable to detect which to learn
or which to keep from
wearing the faces
of our seasonal excuses
constantly lying to each other
and ourselves about just how much
of the daylight
we understand
we would be there:
with the position of our minds
bent towards the autumn fox
feasts
feeling the strength and prayer
of the endured sacred human tests
we would set aside the year's
smallpox dead
whole and complete
with resignation
like the signs from the four legs
of our direction
standing still
sixty years back in time
breathing into the frosted lungs
of our horses the winter blessings
of our clan gods

through dependence
they would carry our belongings
and families to the woodlands
of eastern iowa to hunt our food
separate and apart
from the tribe
following and sometimes using
the river to cleanse the blood
from our daughters and wives
not knowing that far into
our lives we'd be the skulls
of their miscarriages
as a result:
the salamander would paralyze
our voice and hearing
under instruction
our sons the mutes would darken
their bodies with ash and we'd assist
them erect sweatlodges with canvas
water   plants   fire   and   poles
from the river
the scent of deer and geese
the hiss of medicine
against the heated rocks
belief would breathe into their bodies
camouflage and invisibility

somewhere an image of a woman's hand
would lunge out from the window
of a longhouse
and it would grab from our fingers
the secret writings of a book
describing to the appointee
the method of entering
the spirit and body
of a turkey
to walk at night in suspension
above the boundaries of cedar incense
to begin this line of witchcraft
traveling in various

animal forms
unaware of the discrepancy
that this too is an act of balance
a recurring dream of you
being whole and complete
sending the glint of your horns
into the great distances
of the gods
acquainting yourself with ritual
and abandonment of self-justification
to realize there is a point
when you stop being a people
sitting somewhere and reading
the poetry of others come out easily
at random
unlike yours which is hard to write
to feel yourself stretch
beyond limitation
to come here and write this poem
about something no one
knows about
no authority to anything

we are darkness itself

we are darkness
itself

we are sitting
propped against
a wall

we are holding
our knees up against
our bodies

beside us
lies an overturned
figurine

someone advises us
if we hold it
and sing with it

we are preparing
for when we die
its use will be seen

as a spark

going in circles
and there shouldn't
be any misidentification

you are the only one
here

it doesn't matter
if your father
uncle
or brother attends
and shakes the instrument

and sings

the old man with
the beard and metal
glasses
dances with his bowlegs
and hunched back over
the earthen floor

he tells me
for us
it can be too late

through his alcoholic
breath i believe him

the whites can always
catch up with their
belief

if you feel you have
to begin
do so now

or else you will
be forever
in repentance

and when the time comes
after your death
what will you
do when you
are

asked by the *one*
who checks into the past
about your life

and if you followed
what you are supposed
to

i will do as i have
done all my life

i will stand
with my head down

i will shrug my shoulders
declare my love for all
those who went and passed
this way

before me

4
the sound
he makes—the
sound i hear

it seems as if we are so far apart

it has been a steady thing now.
the cars drive by and the houses
and to whom they will be given
becomes a pathetic problem.
i keep looking in magazines.
last night i found an ad for
a chain saw and included
was a mechanical attachment
which enabled one to trim
logs into rectangles.
this would be a house
for us. a log cabin
in the pinetrees.
one room would be enough.
what would it represent?
four symmetrical walls of wood.
small windows.
the daylight coming in
with the morning.

there are two people
who live within those pinetrees.
we are all contrivances.
times when we can never
pinpoint what we are.
most depend on pretenses.

i can't live in ideal situations.
i have fallen off somewhere.
i am doing something which
cannot fit into what i foresee.
i am in balance on top of a frame.

it is a wall on the east side
of a house. i can see the adjacent rooms.
the fresh smell of pine.
sawdust. the strain and the effort
of two shadows.

it seems as if we are so far apart,
living here, in this house we share.
the children who survived the undertakings
of our night-enemy inhabit distant towns.
it still isn't too far.
i am incessantly afraid for them.
i am witness to a nocturnal fire.
small sticks are implanted
in the ground. there is a man stooped
over them, conversing.
on the spot where he is,
i have sensed before there
was some sort of dwelling.
this man has chosen a face
he'll carve from a tree.
as usual the hours pass each day
and i discover myself contemplating
my fate. i somehow seem satisfied
when cars pass on the road
frantically, stopping at each
neighborhood, informing the people
of the drunks who shot and killed
one another. i stand unencumbered
smoking a cigarette.

there will never be an answer
to the individual who wakes up dead.
families rush to other tribal healers.
spells and incantations are congested
with smoke and fire, speedometers,
gas stations, farmland.
the brown stringy root
goes out from the mound
in the earth and tunnels itself

into the tender feet of a girl.
her feet swell. another tunnels
itself into a finger which pulls
a trigger of a gun, independently,
exploding and sending the blood
of someone's son to the stars.
in a distant town, an old emaciated man
reinforces his prayer before the nurses
enter his cubicle, checking the plastic
that holds and nourishes his body.
deaf, he continues his homage
to the guardian bird.
to the nurses, it is simply
entertainment. somewhere else,
a boy gets off an elevator.
two unknown assailants brandishing
knives shove him against the wall.
the skin from his face gently peels
and falls onto the carpeted floor.
the nurse smiles at the old man.

lightning walks along its own path.
the cottonwoods are charred
and as i pass by them before
the sun ascends,
they conjointly point to me
and i can hear their accusations,
blaming me for the death
of a human and a tree.
never place the two together.
i am on this earth for no reason
other than to succeed and to practice
it. people come to me and as their
elder i can ascertain in their discussion
the strong grudge and dislike for all
who surpass them in their ambitions.
i see the young girl who has married
into the family. i sense the minute
sewn-on bundle in the corner
of her printed apron. she,

like the others, has been sent.
there is a man who can change into
a toad. from the north, i see the lights
in the eyes of dwarfs. after
the alcoholics have passed out
in their cars, the dwarfs come out
from the ditches. they brush their
moist hands against the alcoholics'
shiny faces.

i touch a gentle deer

i touch a gentle deer
on the neck with my cold hand.
it informs me of the lines
in the river.
the frozen bait
at the close of october.
from my mother
i hear:

you will never possess
anything if you make
alcohol your being.

you will subsequently
lose whatever else
is left of you.
the tribe has no one

particular characteristic.
none were created from
our creator.

only after and as separates.

like yours
the new cars on the road
are only a hazard for those
who walk or drive

unaware of your
distorted presence.

money is good and it came
in due time, however its origin
and intent. i hope no one finds
pain within this.

the water numbs
my fingers and i have
trouble loading the cylinder
of my pistol.

the cool breeze comes down
along the side of the pinetrees.

i am in favor of the fluctuating
moon.

usually it fades away.
i think of the divisions
within the lives
of people.

i picture triangles
descending from the moon
and they surround people
who consider themselves
different

from the rest.
sometimes there are just
families. sometimes it involves
dependence. a commitment.

once i walk through
these demarcations
it will confuse the moon.
mouths on the somber faces
of people will become rampant.

the owl doesn't call out
again. even though i try
not to think of it,

i see the owl and myself.
the sound he makes.
the sound i hear.

a pool of water, a reflection
of a summer

from the very beginning of the summer,
we sat beside the brown river while it flooded.
we imagined great suspended fish under the rapids
and foam, taking the bait into their mouths
and sending the vibrations of their power
through our lines into our hands.

and the man who gave away dreams died along
with his songs, his memory. the clans.
there was a man who sat beside him,
a student who boasted about his mental
capabilities of remembering the songs
and their sequence. how he could outsing
the old man.

being afraid to see his still presence,
we fished that day. this wasn't the first for me.
it was a time to replace reality with the ardor
of a hunt. the sand from the beach drifted pebble
by pebble into the rushing river.

once when i went to a funeral for two people,
i bid them farewell in english. i wanted to stop
and start over. i felt disconcerted as i walked away
from them, but the line kept moving.
many wanted to put the day behind them.

in the hot misty haze with our barefeet and backs,
we heard what sounded like talk and then singing.
i abandoned the idea of nightfishing,
completely forgot about the fish
who had broken our 30-pound test
three times.

later on, the student of dreams will sit in silence.
no songs will slip into his mind. it will be awkward.
he will only sit there and remember the man who gave
away dreams.

on a bend where once a boat spun itself around
with three men aboard, we sat and i greeted
a snake swimming across, but it quickly changed
direction and came right in front of us.
in an act of appeasement and fear, i threw
my bait, a dead mangled frog, towards its mouth.
it dived and we never saw it again.

i feel it is poetry swimming under the shallow
river. a time imprinted into one's mind:
a last beam of sunset between a valley
of trees filled with hovering birds.
insects darting across the river.
a snake projecting its body from the water
towards your face.

we talked to the ancient paratrooper.
he pointed to the ledge five feet above us:
i used to come here with my brothers,
pulled up a lot of flathead. of course,
it was considerably deeper then.

i remembered hearing my friend speak
of the dynamite blast carrying the water
from the dam up into the sky over the hills.
i wished for some magic to come into us
and to lead us to the fish who chose
to remain behind. fish we would never see.

in viewpoint:
poem for 14 catfish and
the town of tama, iowa

into whose world do we go on living?
the northern pike and the walleye fish
thaw in the heat of the stove.
it wasn't too long ago
when they swam under the water,
sending bursts of water and clouds
of mossy particles from their gills,
camouflaging each other's route—
unable to find the heart to share
the last pockets of sunlight
and oxygen,
stifled by the inevitable
realization that the end is near
when man-sized fish slowly tumble up
from their secretive pits.
i, and many others, have an unparalleled
respect for the iowa river even though
the ice may be four to five feet thick,
but the farmers and the local whites
from the nearby town of tama and surrounding
towns, with their usual characteristic
ignorance and disregard, have driven noisily
over the ice and across our lands
on their pickups and snowmobiles,
disturbing the dwindling fish
and wildlife—
and due to their
own personal greed and self-
displeasure in avoiding the holes
made by tribal spearfishermen in
search of food (which would die
anyway because of the abnormal weather),

the snowmobilers ran and complained like
a bunch of spoiled and obnoxious children
to the conservation officer, who, with
nothing better to do along with a deputy
sheriff and a highway patrolman, rode out
to tribal land and arrested the fishermen
and their catfish.

with a bit of common sense,
and with a thousand other places
in the vast state of iowa to play toys
with their snowmobiles in, and with the winter
snow in well overabundance, they could have gone
elsewhere, but with the same 17th century
instincts they share with their own town's
drunken scums who fantasize like ritual
each weekend of finally secluding and beating
a lone indian's face into a bloody pulp,
they're no different except for the side
of railroad tracks they were born on
and whatever small town social
prominence they were born into.
it is the same attitude shared by lesser
intelligent animals who can't adapt
and get along with their environmental
surroundings.

undaunted, they gladly take our money
into their stores and banks, arrest
at whim our people—
deliberately overcharge us,
have meetings and debates as
to how much they should be paid to educate
our young.
why the paved streets as indicated
in their application for government funds
will benefit the indians.
among them, a dentist jokes and makes claims
about indian teeth he extracted solely
for economics.

the whites will pick and instigate
fights, but whenever an indian is provoked
into a defensive or verbal stand
against their illiterates,
or because he feels that he has been
unjustly wronged for something he has been
doing long before their spermatozoa set
across the atlantic (polluting and bloating
the earth with herbicides and insecticides),
troops of town police, highway patrolmen,
and assorted vigilantes storm through
indian-populated taverns, swinging
their flashlights and nervously holding on
to the bulbous heads of their nightclubs
with their sweaty hands, hoping
and anxiously waiting for someone
to trigger their archaic desires.
state conservation officers enter
our houses without permission,
opening and taking the meat and the skins
of our food from our cooking shacks
and refrigerators.
sometimes a mayor or two will deem it necessary
to come out and chase us and handcuff us over
our graveyards. the town newspaper overpublishes
any wrong or misdeed done by the indian
and the things which are significantly
important to the tribe as well as to the town,
for the most, ends up in the last pages,
after filling its initial pages
with whatever appeals to them as
being newsworthy and relevant indian
reading material.

unfortunately, through all of this,
some of *our* own people we hire, elect,
or appoint become so infected and obsessed
with misconceptions and greed, that they
forget they are there for the purpose
of helping us, not to give themselves

137

and each other's families priorities
in housing, education, and jobs.

altogether, it's pathetic seeing the town
and seeing mature uniformed and suited men
being led astray by its own scum, hiring
and giving morale to its own offspring scum
to make it right for all other scums
to follow.

they can't seem to leave us alone.
until they learn that the world and time
has moved on regardless of whether they still
believe and harbor antiquated ideas and notions
of being superior because of their pale light skin
alone, and until they learn that in their paranoia
to compare us to their desensitized lives,
they will never progress into what they
themselves call a community,
or even for the least,
a human.

it is the fish-faced boy who struggles

it is the fish-faced boy who struggles
with himself beside the variant rivers
that his parents pass on their horse
and wagon. he sees the brilliant river.
at times it turns invisible and he sees
fish he has never seen before.
once, somewhere here he had dreamt
of a wild pig killing his mother and
sister. it chased him into the river
and he swam to the other side and stood
on the beach, wiping the water from his face.
two others came and encircled him.
the dream ended under the river
where he walked into a room
full of people dressed in sacks.
the morning wind chilled his languid body.
he peered out again. birds hopped along
the frosted grass. he remembered what
the submerged people said to him when
he walked into the room: we've been
expecting you.
large glistening fins filled
his eyes with the harsh sunlight.
he felt his lungs expanding.
the ribs from his body tilted
at an angle away from the ground.
the fish in the river, a spectacle.
he sat back against the rocking
sideboards of the wagon.
he noticed his father's black hat
and his mother's striped wool blanket
bouncing in the ride.

as they crossed the iron bridge
he felt the tension from his body
subside. fog from the openings
in the river drifted into the swamps.
the road led them through a forest.
he thought of invisibility.
the web between the bone spines of the fish
were intercrossed with incandescent fiber.
their jaws sent bursts of water
down to the river bottom.
clouds of mud and sediment
settled beside white needlepoint teeth.
he could faintly hear the barking of dogs.
he knew they were nearing home
from the permeating scent
of the pinetrees. it occurred to him
that the trees and the scent were an
intrinsic part of the seasons.
these were moments when he questioned
his existence. for awhile he pictured
awkwardly dressed people. they were standing
motionless beside long tables.
the impression was, they were ready
to eat but there was no food.
he had seen the long tables somewhere.
the wagon stopped. his father stepped
down from the wagon and carried him
into the summer house. it was warm inside.
huge poles which supported the roof
stood in dark brown color absorbing
the constant smoke from the fire.
far ahead in time, his grandson
would come down from the lavender hills
with the intention of digging out the poles
to carry on the memory under a new roof.

he knew it was the next day
when he woke. he could hear the chickens
shuffling about. it was no longer warm.
the daylight dissipated as it came in

through the hole in the center
of the roof.
he turned on his side
and bumped into a small tin bucket.
he reached over and drew it close.
at first smell,
he couldn't define it, but gradually
as he slushed it around, he recognized
his vomit. yesterday's food.
suspended above the door
was a dried head of a fish.
its face a shield. the rainbow-
colored eyes. the teeth were constructed
with blue stone. he knew its symbols
represented a guardian.
white painted thorns and barbs stuck
out from its gills. lines of daylight
rushed through the cracks in the walls.
the smoke-darkened poles were ornately
decorated. the door moved against the force
of the centered breeze. the cool odor
of the pinetrees chilled his entire body.
he pulled his thin blanket closer to him
and he attempted to walk to the door.
for each step he took, he forgot
through the next one. he could faintly
distinguish what sounded like the cracking
of ice over the flapping of wings.

his father stood above the ice
with a spear in his arms. his eyes affixed
to the opening. the giant fish swam by
piled on top of one another. some were
luminous. others swam so close together
they resembled clouds. there were even
a few who quickly swallowed what looked
like intestines. the ones who had their
mouths closed led long streamers
of this substance and it camouflaged
whoever followed behind. these were the fish

who represented a power and a belief.
the season was coming sooner than
anyone had anticipated.
the people in the hills
completely forgot their ceremonies
yet you saw them everywhere, here, to observe.
the women were along the banks
of the river tying long straps
of leather around the deer hooves
on their feet.
the men in their dried speckled
fish heads hummed as they scraped blue
curls of ice with their stone teeth.
small children covered each mark
on the ice. fresh water was refilled.
underneath, the fish swung their tails
side to side, alert.
the women in their deer hooves
walked onto the ice.
the men in their fish heads
began to sing and the small children
after drinking what remained of the water
ran ahead pointing out the giant fish.

in each of us

in each of us
when we look out into the world
it is the same thing
no one tries to be lonely
the limitations are there
for us to confront
throughout our lives
no one questions
the burden
of finding
a solution to why
the occult and the belief
of a changing tribe
mix

i once wrote
of myself in a paper
a circle within a circle
an encounter with the isolation
caused by living beside
the railroad tracks

in a small light-brown house
i sketched out my abstractions
my brother came with the intent
of living with me through
the winter while he worked
loading plastic pipes
into trucks
he stayed for
a couple of nights

one morning i woke up
and i finally found out nothing
could ever be accomplished
there

i walked around on the tile floor
the dull electric light hummed erratically
above me
outside it was raining
i pictured a dying animal
in my mind
it fed on the sickness
it was dying from

i was never old then
it was just nervousness
a feeling as if i would never
have another opportunity
to grasp what represented
an escape from the gradual
settling of my life

i felt my body dissolving
whatever was left of me
floated over a river

the streets were black
from the rain
i blessed the pistol
in the dresser

no one can deny the strong force

no one can deny the strong force
of the river under the ice.
where there are openings,
sheets of ice lift their jagged
bodies up into the wintry air
to take an occasional
but detailed glimpse of us.
we can hear someone amused.
up ahead, we see a glow.
we trudge deeper into the shade
of the willows, of the badger.

the cold stinging wind freezes our eyelids.
we wrap our lips around the willows.
we fall asleep to the sounds
of our backpacks whipping
in repetition across the snowdrift.

each winged object alarms us.
once, there was a venerable name
for each serpent.
everyone with their reasoning intact
carried their belongings on their backs.
water and something to eat.

so much for the thought of surviving
its winter.

we had been raised believing in the omen
of the multi-colored tempestuous badger.
we see the painted scales of the fish
he rides.

the roof above us is similar to his.
spots of light come through
and we stand within the continuous
design of the clouds, wind,
and the sun.

the music we sing represents our struggle.
at first, it is a series and then it
culminates to one total.
from great distances, people arrive
and we are told to respect them
for they have retained the capacity
to cure anything.

we embarrass ourselves by joining
in song with them.
passive moments with them were contradictions.

it makes the people who stayed away
happy. of course, it doesn't mean much.
we are all bonded within the same aspect
of waiting.

even before anything ever became
important, we were living as if we knew
what the reasons were.
children grew around us
and we were told it was important
despite the fact they were fatherless.
some fathers we knew,
others we never met.

each child was different from
its brothers and sisters.

she remembers the room where she followed
the hand of her father
traveling up the walls.
he would be there standing headless
near the ceiling, whistling songs.

146

the hand i followed was old and wrinkled.
it pointed to a bundled object
in the corner.
i remember the dried head
of the fish and there were pictures
on the wall around it,
signifying the mystical world
it came from.

she later realized that she had been
deliberately lied to and that the hand
she followed was a spider.
the same happened to me.
both had nothing to do with what
we were looking for.

we've been told he is persistently evasive
that the river would be the most obvious
place he would be.

we sat up most of the night.
sharpening the barbs of our long spears.
above us, the moon stood in watch.

there were never enough words
associating the badger with the fish
whom we prayed to.

the files made the barbs shine.
in our minds we imagined our spears
digging into his furry neck,
turning the snow and ice red
before its essence reached the ground.

she spoke of the vagueness
in her vision. the animals who
would benefit from this deed.
she sighed with relief and she forgot
what she was talking about when she found
i had already filled the bags and containers
with food and water.

147

medicine for our enervated bodies.

the clock on the wall ticked
and the blanket which was spread out
on the coarse floor made us close our eyes
and we saw pastures filled with apple trees.

the crow-colored man in the green shirt
surprised us when he quickly drew open
the curtains.

the sunlight entered the room in sequences.
i saw the wide-faced man
tearing open the breast of a bird.

he placed its lung on a white handkerchief
and he smeared his face with it.
i saw the tension of his life
on his face recede.
knots of human skin unraveled itself.

he spoke:
the sound of waves on a grey and misty
afternoon is but a fragment
and the pebble which i valued
because it came from the ocean
probably rolls behind me
whenever i walk by drunk
looking for the billfold
it was in.

the rotting flesh of the seal
and the damp sand on the beach
are better thoughts.

for whatever i was worth
and because i heeded instruction,
i released what i brought
in my palm.

148

parts of my life,
parts of everyone's life,
floated away in the foam,
the spit, the regurgitation,
the rebirth of fish.

this is what i gave,
this is what i am.

no one knows the reason why.
no one can ever do anything about it.
it's a long hallway with rooms
filled with dead friends.
the noise of their talking
grows quiet every time
you take a step.

if you persist
you will eventually learn
how to do the right things.

there used to be a path
into the lavender hills where we lived.
in someone's death, i was witness
to the unrecognizable beings who raised me.

i used to see a man comprised of white smoke
and he would take the billfold from his
pocket and i found myself doing the same.

whatever was in those billfolds
radiated.

in the morning i would hear of the man
who died from a hole in his back.
no explanation from anyone.
all the doctor said about him
led to alcohol,
the bottles that were scattered
around him.

i found the pebble beside
a rotting seal.
i thought to myself:
this is where it ends,
where the ocean begins.
this will be the farthest i will ever walk
to all those behind me who can tell me who
i am, where i fit among them.

i see my life collect itself on the foam.
my family drifts by.
my mother and father drilling holes
in the maple tree, my sisters and brothers
carrying silver buckets of sweetwater,
my uncles standing next to each other
huddled over the buzzing chain saw.

i place the pebble in my billfold.
i hear people behind me.
seagulls walk frantically down the path.

the door opened into the bright
moonlight.
the man in the white smoke
stood with his arms gesturing
towards the west.

bubbles collected in the foam,
in old bandages and photographs,
in a pink wooden leg.
i remembered the brown skin of the stout
puffy-eyed man. he would smile in the blue-green
summer air. we danced and stomped with our chests
out and we called out to him in the voices
of grown men. he smiled at us again when we
went back to our young laughs.
greasy fingers, the taste of strawberries
and watermelon.

like a person representing acclimation.
like being somebody to remind somebody
of the tubes in my body,
the expanding of my chest
and my legs hopping through
the daylight in remembrance of a song,
of a people in charcoal,
in dance.

there were times when i realized
after the colors changed on the floor
that the sun was out warming the earth
with its light and that hours earlier,
it passed through the bodies
of all those who knew me,
all those whose names
i brought to the ocean.

i bowed my head among a thousand seats,
facing the gradually appearing snowcapped
mountains in the north.

men in white clothes drove by
on small machines cutting the grass.
all day in bed i thought it was important
that i had been the first one
to walk across the freshly cut lawn.
it was important to know that my dewy tracks
led away from my despair
of always needing someone
around me
to console me
whenever i hear the point
where it seems i'll forget my gift
to the ocean.

the birds are housed in
a small glass house

the birds are housed in a small glass house
and as they eat nonstop
the food disappears

reflections of their fat bellies amuse them
they inspect their fluffy bodies
and i can see they are content
to be trapped inside

below us, the chained dog walks nervously
no school kids to greet and pet him on saturdays
but the ones who do walk by
ignore him and like an asshole begging
for money or a drink
the dog named chilly willy
barks for attention

winos emerge from an alley in los angeles
near chinatown panhandling for dimes
we have but cheese and bread
they accept

the winter for the maladjusted kids has brought
on a new interest instead of staying home
in front of a television set
they now take pains
in their whiteness to explore the wilderness
which sits beside the frozen creek
which runs behind the apartments
and out into the football field

inside the living room i place the squirrel's
head within the crosshairs of a telescopic sight
he goes about within his morning
climbing out to the last dried buds
of the maple tree

i see my slippery fingers
prying open the boiled skull of the squirrel
the delicious beige lines of his brain
rare indian caviar
the trees gently rock and the obese squirrel
relaxes by stretching across a limb
he has stopped the electricity
the kids talk louder and the ice crumbles
under their weight

the other grey birds on the branches cleaned
their feathers as if it was an act
of establishing their boundaries

they sharpened their beaks until they saw the glimmer
of a sun hovering above them in the clouds

there was one blind bird who trotted over
the branches
memorizing each configuration

in the field near by, silhouettes of dashing rabbits
streaked through the dense brush
on the rooftops of the neighborhood
smoke appeared to climb back into the chimneys
flakes of snow gathered on the window sill

i sometimes wonder what we are doing here
living next to all these white people on this hill
it doesn't make sense when you hardly know
anyone and when you do know someone
it's a person who's trying to place him

and yourself into definition
into a role

overall, nothing helps anyone's search

i dream of a kind lady dressed in ironed
clothes and her shiny black hair
rushes by the many rooms of our thoughts
she walks into some when we are sleeping
she can't help herself
too many thoughts
in one house

on a parched mint-green stationery
i am fond of the poem sent to me
written by luyu
of rain-drenched mountains
excited neighbors

i see her by the window and she thanks the *one*
who delivered the snow
she compares the pitch-black night
to the nights of winter with the light
from the snow illuminating
whatever was visible

the occupants of the house sometimes questioned
themselves in the morning as to whether or not
they heard sounds of someone leaning over their beds
the two younger brothers blamed alcohol
one girl thought it had to do with the baby
she lost years before
the father of the girl looked at himself
in the mirror and he cursed the clan
of her daughter's husband

the painted baskets on the wall
along with the egyptian hanging vibrated

to the warm breeze of the heater

i sketched out a picture of a man
the room of his mobile home had broken windows
glass was lying all around the floor
and he had a gun pointed to his foot
after all this time
he had just learned he was just
as different as his wife was
but more bone-like

i had no way of telling he was drunk
and delirious
i had no way of telling of the gentle fawn
who would nurse his wounds
listen to his lies

in whose memory do we see a young man fighting
his mother

his uncles helped him hide his whereabouts
there was a girl in blue ski pants
washing dishes and her glasses were shaped
like butterflies
she stepped back when the fighting began
the vision of a dying rabbit
struggling within its own blood in the snow
flashed vividly in her mind

how do we catch this and hold it

later explain how we came upon the crossing
of our lives

i value the obsession with tranquil colors
and the damp smell of the spring wind
the helpless souls and the sound of crickets
and the moonlight which absorbs all our actions
all of our pain and decadence

he is each person from each season
with different faces of denial and rejection
the design of yellow pears on the curtains
will fade in the constant sunlight
it makes sense to remain inside
to think of it as being necessary
to sit here on this chair
watching the automobile smoke
spiral up past the trees

like a snake the wind picks up
the snow and swirls it around our windows
icicles plunge to the ground

as the hours pass in this day
mist covers the glass
the frozen earth
the frozen snake

we are held in suspension like the life
forms under the earth in the mud

we are under the constant resolution that
we have overcome all obstacles of learning
nothing else is hidden
by simplicity and by spirit

whatever argument we have for living
has been set aside by those who truly believe
in the capability of the mind
to make it possible to carry on
with the act of recollection

the dark shell which covers us
is a resting eyelid

and we are in its liquid
we tell each other of the time gone by
most of us have no purpose although we are encouraged
to think so

i can still picture the caribou

how far away from death do we imagine ourselves
to be?
is it something to be thought of
from day to day
like the portrayals of lives
on television that people watch,
filling their monotonous and dreary lives?
when my time comes
for participation in anything,
i sense that i will be in a confined state
of mental illness. a lost soul.
an animal who runs back and forth
over the beach,
desperately missing the scent
and the shadows of the people who raised him.
a mental block of my absolute helplessness.
the trouble with me is,
i can't go on pretending
nothing else is needed
to back up your character,
your presence, anywhere.
i have grown into a world
of people pointing and accusing
other people of each other's incompetence
and uselessness.

i am the angle of a secluded corner,
of a closet, of light
disappearing into light.
through my life ahead,
i picture surgeons
standing around me.

we have asked them if there will be complications
with your one lung.
they told us they can't tell us anymore.
go ask again just to see they're not lying.
they said the same thing again.
the coarse paint on the wall
divides itself into another shade.
white and black electric cords
pulsate under the sunlight on the floor.
silver knobs sit on various machines.
the suited man on television talks
about the need to preserve alaska.
caribou migrations. salmon and the brown bear.
mated eagles in the snowfall.
let's save the fucking things.
they're comparable to the migrations
of the wildebeest in africa.
when it finally came
to the point of closing the curtains,
one of the doctors came in
and asked me if it was all right
for them to throw away my lung
like garbage.

as the sun was going down, the red car
raced through the stone-smooth highways
of the endless farmland.
patches of snow regathered the cold
from the shadows in the ditches.
the low rumble of the mufflers
grew quiet as the car passed over
the iron bridge.
below them, the frozen river
ran through the passengers' lives
like thoughts.
like a syringe collecting
blood. our mind. this open wound.
out from the clouds,
though invisible, there are vines
as thick as tree trunks,

coming down from the sky,
entangling us.
this is how we sometimes
know where we are being led to.
the people you meet are accidents.
we like to think
otherwise.
once those tree trunks found
the three of us passed out
in a junked car.
it was the middle of january
and when we woke we arranged our bodies
as if we were going for a ride.

seventy-five years ago, our places
were probably filled with dance
and constant prayer.
breath made of the day's
offering instead of alcohol.
alcohol made us dream of the car's
green interior lights.
the surgeons may keep their secrets
as long as the one lung keeps me.
let it be so important to them.
to the west, the animal
has stood on its hindlegs,
exhausting himself,
looking for something which will eventually
be lost.
the beach is dotted with his chaotic tracks.
the polluted seagull flies out from the waves
over the rolling ocean.
his feathers are packed together.
his imagination is as good
as anyone's.
he dreams of a swim
into the curling waves.
telephone calls bring police
to the ten tons of weapons
we buried.

we listen for stories
and read papers, novels, but everything ends
up the same, either dead, barely living,
or else there are senseless men with clubs
killing off the young harp seals,
the porpoise.
it started with the buffalo
and now because hunters shoot too much
caribou, wolves are shot from helicopters.
in the white man's own stupidity,
bear is still hunted in montana.

of course, nothing is new.
the actors within all of us keep us going.
the animals have no actors.
tuna fleets have been suspended
for two months. they think this will solve
the problem of the porpoise.
we walk into a room and we listen
to the educated man talk about his paranoia
of eventually living until his grandchildren
no longer resemble his race.
the world will consist of grey people
with grey gods.
many will try to revert.
they will choose any origin.
death will be anybody's choice.
if a baby is asked whether he chooses
life or death, there must always be someone
present to represent the baby.
the symbol that we will live by
will be a legless and headless man.
paintings and collages will always express
the desires of simplicity.
windowless houses and buildings.
no mirrors, glass, or refractions.
work and food will be small.
no mention of pay or anything
financial.
because one of us cared enough

160

not to see the other suffer
through comparisons,
one of us left.
my call out to the hallway
went unanswered.

the eventual death of the animal on the beach
made us aware of each other's
capabilities.
i was one of the carpenters' helpers
sweating in the lush green valley.
the rushing water from the creek
sometimes sounded like dishes
banging against each other.
dust from the passing cars
and trucks settled over our eyebrows.
someone said something about meat decaying
and the sound of hammers started over again.
the fat man in overalls carefully
tape-measured the length
of the room and he paid particular
attention to the dimensions
of the four corners.
he scribbled out his equations
on the pinewood.
grey river birds honked through
the treetops.
the red sun found us thinking
over the thoughts that once slowed
our lives. the young seal's coat shimmers
under the neon lights of new york.
i am disappointed at how many people
are killed by the great white shark.
there should be more.
red triangles within the chest cavity.
there's no special reason.
it's just an unwanted day.
the red car returns over the bridge.
and the call i made out to the hallway visibly
turns into small black letterings.

in the sleep and darkness of my skull,
i can still picture the caribou,
running alongside a green moist hill
with its antlers raised up towards the sky.
with clouds, everywhere.

after the fourth autumn

for e

it
like almost any
other anachronism
in my existence
is a test
and on the sides
are people
curious
on finding out
how and when i'll die
we pretend we're
related
and that when
we hear of the young
sister's disapproval
of the baby
melissa
i resolve
the bitch in

question
grew promiscuous
long before us
she will never surpass
or outgrow her
woman things

for the rain in march:
the blackened hearts of herons

i see myself sleeping
and i see other ignorant people
locked securely in their houses
sleeping
unaware of the soft dawn-lit
furbearing animals
wrapping themselves with the bark
and cone from pinetrees
within each of their thoughts
there is the vision
of the small muskrat's
clasped hands
the struggling
black and yellow
spotted body of a salamander
freeing itself from a young
girl's womb

in my dark blue pickup
i came upon a cigar-smoking
badger
who invited himself and
later came to my home
gathering chips and splinters
of my firewood and starting
a fire
for an hour we sat
and then he suddenly stood
on his hindlegs and walked
over to the stove
and opened it
he took out two narrow pieces
of burning wood and rammed them
into his eyes
he fell on all fours
and then made rumbling sounds
mocking my pickup with its two
dull headlights
disappearing into
the forest

i dream of a painter
in the desert who tells me
his twisted and contorted
paintings of indians
amuse him because it's
the type of stuff whites buy
and enjoy
how i guess they still see us
because his family once helped
the spaniards build missions
in california
at least he knew his parents
were indians
that's what the old man
in the field kept telling us
flower petals crumbled through
his fingers

but we already know how the cycle
goes
the trees and the weeds
quickly grow and decay
in the reflection
of his sunglasses
his lips and teeth are still
stained with coffee and tobacco
the cross-eyed boy
smirked at his remarks
he was impressed
with the mountains anyway
not the seeds that went into
the earth
not with the man-sized fish
who waited each spring
for the river ice
to break up
to feed on the offerings
of miscarriages
he was told and experienced
all in one night
somewhere in canada
the cactus and the medicine
they called peyote
deep inside that night
he thought he knew and he probably
sat through the whole two-day ride
back to chicago thinking he was
truly indian
he probably thought it
right up until the moment
he pissed and examined
his shriveled body
in the showers
seeing and feeling for the last time
the bitter green liquid

within each of our lives
as we are growing we are given

and we experience these choices
but it isn't until later after we have
filled ourselves with bowls and bowls
of another food that we realize we have
chosen the wrong side
i know it will be the same for me
for there was a time last week
when i forgot to bring alive
into someone's mind
a hand reaching into hot boiling
water
a ball of fire bouncing
in front of the yard
in my childhood i can remember
what it felt like to feel the power
and mass of a ship i later recognized
as a spanish galleon
everytime i vomited into
the light-green lard can
i saw the underside of this
ship
sailing past the man who
called to me
he sat back against the black
cardboard wall and whenever he smiled
i could see his coarse white hair
his yellow fingernails

the next time i saw him
a bald-headed hooked-nosed man
in overalls stood in the brilliance
of the summer daylight
the bright green grass reflected
on the linen and the dishes shined
and the aroma of chicken and corn
filled the nostrils of people
and the mangy dogs who were my pets
watched from under the porch
he will stand in the place
of your grandfather

166

your grandfather will watch
this day pass through
his eyes
years later he sometimes waved
to me on the road as he drove back
from his soybean fields
he would stand on his tractor
i never knew what he said to me
that one day under the apple tree
when he stood in replacement
of my grandfather
i was too busy thinking
about the middle-aged man
who lifted up the sleeping girl's
dress that morning:
he was laughing but it sounded
more like grunting
i had just woke and it seemed
like he had been standing over the girl
waiting for me to open my eyes
because the blankets had been moved
to one side of her
he pointed under the dress
he touched and then he clowned and mimicked
and then hobbled out of the house
with a barrel of dishes

from then on whenever i saw him
he did his clown act which always
left me humored
but i will never forget one fall night
ten years ago when the sound of a pheasant
brought us together
through his song i watched
the day and night split in half
inside the electric lightbulb
and through each motion
of my mind and body
i saw a birchtree give birth
to snowflakes

there was a horse
and then a man
they each divided portions
of themselves and then they walked
away as one
the next day without any night's rest
i chopped wood for my grandmother
all afternoon
i imagined the wood as being things
i wanted to go rapidly behind me
there was no room for the mother
who shot her son in the neck
no room for the man who said
he'd pull the trigger on the lives
of six people
all lined up in a row
unless it was completely understood
why he came back

through the screen over the opened
window i felt the small hands
of a toad examining my round
face
the hammock moved within
the toad's breath and when he
walked away boils grew over the places
where it had touched me
it was later explained to me
that i was born the same moment
a baby strangled on its own cord
several miles away
so now whenever i stand in front
of a mirror
i go over the small star-shaped
scars
and tell myself that i will
always be afraid of all those born
before me
i listen for the whippoorwill

directing dwarfs to the place
where they will find cigarette butts
the rubber tires of the automobiles
crunch against the rocks
on the road
through the rubble of the fire
of the old blind man's house
all they found was his pink
wooden leg

my mother spilled a box of bullets
on the table
she placed one into an empty coffee can
and poured several capfuls
of grey ash into it
from the window
sparks and the retort of the rifle
spiraled into the blackened hearts
of herons
we looked into the forest
and we saw the silhouette of a pickup
the occasional dim red glow
of someone smoking
it was us in our life ahead
i will never know who i actually am
nor will the woman who lives with me
know me or herself or the children
we want
i am always surprised at how many
different minds drift across
each other
some resenting everyone
some imitating what they will
never be
others make room for others
and then there are us
afraid of everyone because they
are afraid of us
unable to fit anywhere

although we live in apartments
we take weekend drives and visits
to our land with the idea
of getting away from our frustrations
we find ourselves confronted
because of our unity
sisters and aunts blab
within their drinks
when we enter the skidrow taverns
as if they had sat in complete boredom
with nothing to discuss
until they saw us
ordering a couple of beers
from the corner in the dark
restoring everyone's indignation
towards us
we shrug our shoulders
thinking it isn't as bad as trying
to outstare the whites all weekend
but it is
rednecks press their fat longhaired
faces against the window counting us
and i reach into my coat
setting my pistol's safety catch
into fire
it is their daily fantasy
while pouring cement into foundations
or else while scattering cowshit over
the fields of their fathers
to think of themselves finally
secluding me and beating me with their fists
and it is my fantasy to find myself
cornered by four of them
to see the sparks
of my automatic
flashing under their hairy bellies
sirens of police cars and ambulances
whine through the brick alley
they question me
and i tell them it was self-defense

a story they never believe or get tired
of hearing
but the big redhead thinks different
i knew these boys
they wouldn't jump anyone
he turns around and i place
the cold barrel of his .38
behind his pink ear
i squeeze the trigger
and the brain explodes
and splatters everywhere
on the white panel of the ambulance
i create the design and the painting
of his life
i walk away from the wet black streets
of the country town
thinking of my painting
the salamander spearfishing
in the coldest day of winter
for dead fish

coming back i read the poem pow-wow
written by w. d. snodgrass after
visiting my people's annual tribal
celebration
you can't get away from people
who think what they see
is in actuality all they will
ever see
as if all in one moment they can sense
automatically what makes a people
what capabilities they have of
knowledge and intellect
he was only shown what was allowed
to be shown
what the hell did he expect
out of his admission fee?
and as far as he thinking that he knew
more about indians than they themselves did
he should have thought twice

it's the same way with the poem
i am a sioux brave, he said in minneapolis
by james wright and countless others
he will never know the meanings
of the songs he heard
nor will he ever know that these
songs were being sung long before
his grandfathers had notions
of riding across the ocean
long before translators
and imitators came
some claiming to be at least a good 64th
grabbing and printing anything
in scrapbook form
dedicating poems to the indian's loss
writing words and placing themselves
within various animals they knew nothing of
snodgrass will never know what spirit
was contained in that day he sat above
the feathered indians
eating his hot dog

he saw my people in one afternoon
performing and enjoying themselves
i have lived there 26 years and although
i realize within my life i am incomplete
i know for a fact that my people's ways
aren't based on grade-b movies
and i also know that the only thing
he will ever experience in life
as being phenomenal
will be his lust
stirring and feebly coming alive
at the thought of women
crumbs from the bread
of his hot dog
being carried away
by images of crushed
insects

my father speaks to us
as we sit in the living room
he is in the other room
sketching in detail the face of his father
he'll be there for several days
and we won't see him
we have gone back for the weekend
again
nothing changes
there's not much i can say
to the indian who beats other indians
he lives in his long trailer thinking
he has finally settled into
the land he hardly knows
thinking he will forever
be a man even if my brother and i
make his face bruised and swollen
nothing seeps into people like him
sitting here i can see
his teethmarks on my knuckles
and he has vowed to me
the only thing which will separate us
is death
between coming here to this desk
and going outside this apartment
for fresh air
i spend my time throwing my fists
in rapid succession toward the mirror
i have always been confident with myself
ever since i entered the boxing ring
in des moines years ago
i used to think i was an asshole
stepping into the canvas and now it's
no different
i am training for a fistfight
which will be fought in an alley
or out on some country road
against a drunk whose honor
i offended
i didn't make it easy for my father

as my grandmother had told me to
friday night
leave your ill feelings outside
the house
or else you will disturb
or push against him
what he is looking for
while my sisters take turns
combing my mother's hair
we hear him talking within
his room shelling kidney beans
we are with him on his walk
through the fog with wilbur
his nephew
checking the traps along
the river
on the way back they see a young
dismembered body of a girl
scattered for a quarter of a mile
they do not talk to each other
through the whole stretch
of the railroad tracks

a man comes to us
and he greets us and we exchange
kind words with him but we are puzzled
when we find after he has left
that we are still thinking about him
i place a hand in my pocket
and i touch and feel one single bean
for an evening we sit
trying to figure out how
the man placed it there
for each block and section
of color or a shade which
comes close to it
he divides them into several
of the more luminescent ones
the black paint of the tempera
outlines our features

174

shadows are layers of color
going from darkest to lightest
dead fish pile on top
of one another and the snow
continues towards spring
before the frogs sing
furry-shaped men light their fires
as they wake in their caves
a handsome man paddles by in his boat
and the three women on the shore
of the river frantically wave their arms
to him but he ignores them and he goes
downriver
he is bothered by the thought
of flashing minerals
dates and calendars
how the times remind
him of *the russian*
messenger

march twenty-eight/1977

my finger is still numb
and it's been five days now since
for no reason it started to swell
and upon our observance it twisted
and touching it
one could hear and feel
the crunching of small delicate bones
when i went to
the next room to show it
to someone other than
my wife, it took its
normal shape
no discoloration
that next morning we went
to the ditch behind the mailbox
where my hand searched the ground
for our cigarettes
we saw the young plant there
standing on the exact spot
where we thought it would be
my finger could have brushed
against it
or else its essence
was extracted by the incorporeal
and that what happened was supposed
to happen
the two dogs who visited us
the transformation of a giant rabbit
hopping a hundred yards
with wings surfacing on its back
lifting its bird body
to the night on its last hop

whatever is growing now over
the earth
there is so much strength behind it
i see it as a counteracting force
between the points of two knives
knowing that when one slips
it will go through my heart

poem one

it begins with the unfolding vision
of a man swinging his head and neck
like a chicken swallowing water
convulsively
the perfect regurgitation
of a copper tube
how it formed an o
as it came up
in his mouth
before he took it in his hands
rolling and cupping it
singing and spitting upon it
sewing with it like a needle
through canvas through
the patient's knee

when it was time to sleep
i turned the blankets over

to lie down but it was interrupted
by beads of cold water that i felt
on my left shoulder
earlier a garbage bag
collapsed by itself

fifty miles south
a fire appeared across a stream
by my relative's house
a hand touched the screen
farther south
it was associated that
the recent brother who hung
himself in an oklahoman jail
was in effect lonely for the unexplained
hanging of his brother who was home
on leave from the marines
relatives had been outside and below
the walls of his cell window
it was said that voices
were heard in english
voices that weren't supposed
to be there
he was a singer who i thought
was a part of who i wanted
around me to listen to
and now since i know he was death
i trudge behind him
perplexed when bruises appear
over his suicidal face

even though our vision was limited
we could see into the ground fog
and haze above us
we stood hoping the geese
would come towards our way
as soon as they appeared
i let out a shout
and they swerved northward

we started firing our rifles
we knew it was too far

later as we walked on
i regretted firing upon them
it was stupid
immediately i thought
of the pistol i carried inside
the compartment of the nova
ever since pickups started
chasing me on highways
and mainstreets
it was strictly there
to defend us
i didn't know what comparisons
to make and resolve due to my
feelings of respect for the geese
my dependence on the pistol

there were the human-colored feet
of silver squirrels
that later hung on our belts
in the sunlight
i carefully observe
the grey-blue fog in your eyes
along the border of your pupil
the mechanic-like instrument
the dotted purveyor and restorer
of our daily encompassment

it isn't known yet whether
there is a cure for the deafness
in my brother's left ear

both men who can "see"
have verified the cause
attributed to the accidental
brush against menstruation
by the cup used
or the mouth kissed

she wishes for someone to leave
the innards for the owl outside
perhaps it's just hungry
i am thinking it's probably why
he comes each night
the summer is gone anyway
sheets of ice have formed
over the stream and along
the rims of the puddles
on our driveway
laborious insects tunnel their way
deeper into the dead trees
they are similar to spirits
retreating for the winter
their arms are retracted
except for the one finger
which searches about
feeling for signs of frost
scratching the dirt
taking in only enough
to cover them

having dragged the shell
of my house

it wouldn't make sense to anyone anyway
so i figure there's no use trying
to impair someone's daily monotony
by recording mine

i haven't felt it much
the only thing i want is for things
to go well
and for me to confess
to the one who'll see
if there is anything wrong
w/me

i observe the red white-eared deer
standing under the sunflowers
i sense women locked
in confrontation
she
in her soiled clothes
her words are hate
for my protégé
who wears a wig
a persistent target
of physical attacks

it wasn't because of her
hitting her
it was because the other one
mistook that she was being
challenged

actually your sister was doing motions
of her head and hands emulating
the antics of a psychopath

hopefully we listen to the same songs
on the radio
a precarious judgment
for a day which in our thoughts
has begun a seed of our reflections

as i blink my eyes twice
this spring
two humans pass into the world
of death several miles
apart on a highway

the leftover food in the garbage
bags moves by itself
chimes ring inside the plaster
wall

the painting of a brown oval-faced
girl came out from the closet
and it now sits under the table

the green wind of the trees
in the sunlight shines through
the teapots and the fruit

small birds swerve their bodies
in between the chained barking dog
and the tangle of black electric wires

poem for november

first there is the natural
but from this: who & how many can actually
touch
the traveling desolate
speck of dust
representing someone's
path
when we believe it
to be an act of rebirth
which exists in chosen blood only, otherwise
it is memory
an abandoned shadow
casting its last imprint
over us
or a call
from another spectrum where
i am the earth
resulting in warped
generations from
a seal's anxiety in a circus
to swim on a hot
summer day combined with
an unintentional stare at a funeral
descended through
the fiber and tissue
of our developing womb & left us
a dent in our ears and lips
incredulous and reticent
with nothing to sustain even the ordinary
and the times

when i am fortunate
enough to reaffirm
my hands and request
into a distant lucid spark
of two rocks
igniting a dry nest
the blind
pigmentless salamander
knows i am close
to seeing

poem for december

you know we keep coming
across one another
even though we give
the impression
people other than ourselves
can't exist
because of our tribal names
who is and isn't related to us
what harm or influence
you have brought
upon someone
that at times you hear
the high-pitched drone
in your ear

just how much you
understand of yourself
tests are given
common humans who share
the isolation of this
daylight
judge the eligibility
of my chances after death
many people utter my name
in disgust
hopefully some are in favor
of the indian vet
who calls himself a man
who i keep having encounters with
through the radio he receives
the message
he sees me as the viet cong
send the word up ahead
look it up in
flashback: regression of self
i'm supposed to be dead

poem two/rainbow

what remains is the singular black man
sitting in his curtain-
drawn room
quiet and unchanged
even though i have disturbed
his gaze into the lights and dials
of his stereo
i only know him because he has offered
to translate my poems en español
i call my adviser who is his teacher
and he says
"i'd hold back on this if you're
considering publishing
i'd get someone who's sensitive
with the language"
but it was only a deal to help him
with his grade
as a result of his query
on the origins of my camouflage coat
he starts talking:
search and destroy
that was our task
sharpshooter for the tanks
i put 50 slugs in this one cat man
i am murietta
you mean you were in nam?
how old are you?
22?
and you were in the marines?
two years? 74 and 76?
he gets frustrated because i doubt
him
i try to resolve the matter

by rationalizing that acquaintances
died there too
that when my lottery number
came up in 69
i was surprised but a physical
reduced my chances of going 100%
didn't tell him of the times
i sat banging my bony fists
into my knee
seven years after surgery
i ask him about the button
which he gave me the other day
which i promptly refused
after seeing it inside the baggy
soft
fresh and moist with its liquid
dark chalky green
patterns of islands
entrapment
even through the plastic

i told him i only consumed
dry stuff
he laughed and asked if i ever
smoked it
i told him yes
how did it feel?
i felt mostly out of place
he laughed again
that was yesterday evening
the cactus is drying by the window
webs of cottony strychnine
my chapped hands are chilled
from the november wind
in his eyes he has the look
as if he had just extricated himself from
a woman
i'm sorry i came in
all i wanted was a nickel
thanks for the cigarette
anyway

three reasons for transgression: the fierce head of the eagle, the otter, and the daylight

1.

i have lost you completely now
nothing brings back memory
of you or of me having anything
to do with you
we keep hearing you scream
in your weekend drunkenness
that you don't give a shit
anymore
bored by your obsession
the other drunks
sensing impermanence
have no alternative
than to agree with you
they ride in packs
looking for me
having things turn around
on them
they found themselves
under our fists
don't ever contest me
in courts
you would lose
if i shot you
in front of your house
i would go free within
a month
no one would care
about the outcome
if i went and shot
the other half who's

just as crazy
i'd still go free
that in itself is strange
but it's true
the man who is walking
75 miles away
is testimony to this
lucky him
going to school
(anymore he isn't satisfied
to at least be able to walk
in the daylight to know he's left
behind sticks for what resembled
a son to his father
another son to whom he feeds
naming the name of the other
who floats by like a speck
of dust)
and me
i continually receive letters
from a big-assed white
informing me of the tribe's
depleted education funds
maybe so
but i perceive an indian
who has returned from failing
acculturation in the city
sticking it to her
telling her what to tell me
of how much time i am allotted
to complete school
i am unaffected
i hold readings and workshops
for subsistence
i try to refrain from several topics
as if an aura of magic
encompassed them
and with each word i would lose
parts of a sequence of thought
of an otter swimming and taking food

in its mouth to a dejected person
on a small sandy island
the buds on the trees outside
this apartment are light green
and the birds sing all night
and the air is filled
with the rapid movements
of earth and people
i feel i am growing stronger
whenever i stand in front
of them
what do you do when there is a man
who represents your dreams
who goes talking and appraising
his deeds
and for no reason he stops
and says something new
there is a chance
for those who want to learn
but not for those who feel it
hard and difficult
that's the way it's been for me
i leave alone the thought
of an old movie house
and we twitch our necks
to laughs that aren't there
when we look
listening to the tape recorder
last night
something brought back
the memory of lodge grass, montana
a tribal member who had married into
the people
focused his eyes on me
as he sat and sang with a drum
composed with unfamiliar faces
we were locked into four separate
social structures
we knew we didn't fit
no matter how much impression we gave

doesn't matter really
the fact is
today he'll be buried
the memory of him enlarged
like a photograph
twice last night
i never thought it was important
until i opened the papers
this morning to read his services
will be held today
i think i've got to let
the pet rabbit go
i've got to let myself go
my teeth are tired of chewing
the masking tape which bonds
and cages us
outside it's as if
the weather's acting in accord
but the green buds on the treetops
are alive
they think different
they're not in objection
they are glad
the brittle glass cup
filled with coffee speaks to me
when i touch it for a drink
and i immediately sense
i have no need for answers
i'll always accept myself

cedar falls: the spinster
in political science

2.

no matter where i have stood
and sat within the past three days
i keep getting headaches

there were times when i would walk
across the campus on a hot afternoon
with blood spurting from my nose
and i would gag on clots
trying to hold my composure
i nod my head and agree
with the lighting stella offers
i feel the strain in my eyes subside
i hear the chimes on the curtain bar ring
i'm tired of smoking
i'm tired of drinking
i'm nervous in front of company
or else i run out of goddamned things
to talk about
i have nothing in common with anyone
it confuses circumstances even more
when instructors mention that something
would be terribly wrong if in their excavations
they found a rusted computer among
the american indian
why a black thought it was racist
of the associations made as english
being a common bond of a polity
that the black said it wasn't
because he could communicate
with any indian by walking up
to one and saying how
of the little squinty-eyed man
whose karma was once spilled
on the eastern front in the form
of a german officer's blood
how this one particular person
knows someone in the dept. of the interior
who said *they* wouldn't waste their fucking time
if they wanted to utilize indian lands
for resources
characters like these play rough
to keep minorities down
places like gordon, nebraska
dead naked indians in dancehalls

it doesn't say much for what
they're trying to teach me
we came home because of my headaches
it's saturday night
the coffee is boiling
it reminds me of the rain
that fell this evening
it reminds me of two people
uttering and questioning
a person's name
the pinetrees bend and twist
above them
they chose to forget the name
to walk out safely from the woods

he writes
i try to be unconcerned about
the black doe-fawn council's decision
to accept a city indian's application
for overseer
maybe i'm doing it all wrong
although i have told myself
if the possibility ever arose
my being asked to take the job
i would turn it down
because of my self-doubt
as to how i would do publicly
with my mind in complete bilingual
awareness
able to verbally construct an opinion
and to substantiate my decisions
with knowledge and truth
experience with the past
and the past previous
on the inside i have nothing
to support the individual i am
at least that's how i see
a leader to be
not a joker
not anyone who feels

he wants to "help" on the spur
of a moment
those are the kind who hide
in their houses or else the kind
who come back after living in the city
for 20 or 30 years
i should plan on living there
for a long time
instead of wasting my time
on the pretense of getting my degree
and if things are as they are now
i will have no trouble obtaining
any kind of position
my simple white restraintless being
will pay for itself
they'll probably even build
a house for me as they have done
for her as to the man
who gave her the job gave himself
a house did
doesn't matter how much indian
i try to be
fact is
i have a better chance
if i become a white or a wino
for two-thirds of my life

it doesn't hurt to criticize further
closer to our origins
if he feels we are incapable
of holding the job then reluctantly
i don't have much faith with them
although they probably believe otherwise
they have illusions that they can sit
and at will outthink and outwit
each white representative that comes along
bringing documents and explanations
showing them the government's ways
of finding propensities
and solutions

to build and make use of tribal land
they can't understand everything
if i am having trouble
they are the same
it's not a matter of who has better
mental capabilities or comprehension
or who is the self-made man
what power he has or thinks he has
truth is
some of us go through life
like the fierce head of an eagle
perpetually deceiving the other man
mentally constructing a death
an injury or a sway
in how we wish the future to turn
when he transgresses our accomplishments

even though the flood
made the serpent grateful
for the scores of young catfish
who frantically swam along the growth
of the river's edge
the serpent regretted the day ever starting
he would die with his mouth wide open
spines from the catfish protruded
through his skin and muscle
behind the base of his skull
the lodged catfish spoke to him
inside his throat:
i like to tell people when
they are making assholes
out of themselves
there was nothing in your blood
no reason for the world to begin
that said *you* should make decisions

within the past few days
whatever belongs to me
has tumbled and turned
insidious

and my feelings pour out
into the darkness
of my chest cavity
old habits return like a parasitical
shadow who left years ago
and now returns through the window
which it purposely left open
as we dream
we accidentally place our fingers
through our chest
and into our hearts
we touch and feel it
talking to us:
it's up to you to define
what your name is
whose body it once wound itself
around
i was fresh from the womb
i never made it a point
to hate anyone
i question the incineration
of human flesh
that's the difference
to have doubt

in the early hours of the morning
we remember bits of conversation
but the idea of it overwhelmed us
even though we didn't understand it
it had to do with a disposal of a human
it had already sided with us
by the time thunderheads
began to show through the dawn
to the north
my wife had just loaded the pistol

we heard the jingle of his keys
as he walked to his car trunk
the last time i saw him
he was sliding the bolt

of his carcano against the barrel
i saw the gold gleam
of the bullet casing
i grabbed the pistol from her hands
and i began firing just as soon
as he rounded the car
his rifle discharged
after four of my bullets
struck him in the chest and face
twigs from the thorn tree
fell into the river
i got off the car
and went over to his body
and asked him if he had any beer
i took what he had in the trunk
and whatever drunks and winos
he had in his car
were glad to ride along
with us

3.

when i think of the process you have
unnecessarily gone through
of bearing a child
i don't know how it feels
even though i have tried
to understand at depth
the category in which fools
like us fit

in the end
there is no difference
the child grows
we slobber and blurt out
his name through the foam
of the beer
our wine-spotted clothing
born through years of alcoholic vision

we argue what his indian name means
when the best times occurred
why it was essential with each
person met to foretell him
the time of your death
times when we woke in our houses
with the wind inside
the windows all busted
relatives who didn't belong to us
we pass from car window
to car window
a printed sheet for his
shivering body
his father can barely speak
to us but we are reluctant to take
the baby from his father
he tells us the car won't start
and we assure him by saying
that if we see his wife
in town we'll tell her
to hurry with the gas
as we drive off
we look into the rearview mirror
and we see the baby instinctively covering
himself with the sheet
later we see his mother
being led to a silver pickup
by three fluorescent-hatted farmers
chapped hands and palms lined
with pigshit
strong talk among the guts
of headless catfish

we ask ourselves
if in effect we are anywhere
close to where we're supposed to be
if in fact the concept of learning
has been worth it
if it isn't by genetics alone
that i go around

reading and teaching
what's left
and what i've absorbed
i tell the students
of sidewalks and factory-centered
towns
of the poison produced and distributed
by their white fathers
through the rivers
and waters
of the poison their babies
will suck through the breasts
of their mothers
no one cares to know
some of them will eventually
grow insecure whenever
their supposed dominance
is threatened
telephone calls will be made
policemen take punches at me
even after i tell them it was me
the pickups were chasing
it's inevitable
there was the time we stopped
at wall drug, south dakota
i have no objection
to the commercialized springwater
we drank there but i hate the memory
of how i drove for miles disgusted
with the deliberately placed clumps
of human hair in our hamburgers
some of which we had already eaten
it's strange to check each thing
we buy now because of impressions
left
so much for the badlands

naturally we think it's good
to be on the auspicious side
when we see people suffer around us

and we amuse ourselves
with news of their silly acts
children are thrown
from cliffs into
the ocean

i once drew a picture
of a girl in pencil
who had lived inside a small box
inside the closet of her parent's home
for fourteen years
it reminded me of a rotten frog
who had somehow lived through the night
with half its body spread over
the hot sunlit highway
moss from the swamps
entangled itself to the lower
exposed organs and fibrous tissues
assorted insects flew about
and the frog blinked at each
passing car

from morning star press
and other letters: 1978

the irregular pigmentation
on her skin
is a sign
that a thunderbird
is assisting her

we exist
and for each ongoing moment
regardless of where we are
ageless guardians of all shapes
and dimensions
be they animals or spirits
of past humans
dieties
who are natural
in our blood
they are our sentinels
revolving around us
but what were they thinking
fifteen years ago
when i sat openmouthed
in a dentist's cushioned chair
when over the radio
was broadcast the prediction
of the world coming to an abrupt end
at 3:30
the next day

my mother and uncle comically
thought its revelation was the main reason
instead of the usual pains of tooth
extraction that i lay idle with tears

but discreetly i was glad for not
having to go out and chop
the wet firewood
even though that evening
taps my my diligent foundry-breath
father urged me to get off my ass
but an explanation savored
with the aroma of pork hocks
and potatoes
stopped his rationale

i heard the crunching
of his voracious jaws against his teeth
and he complimented in reluctance
the mist on the window from the warm tea
distant glaciers broke apart
a vulture having sculptured
the land with its wings and body
risking its once beautiful plumage
sat bewildered
thinking it would have been simpler
to have been the chickadee
females hear as they near their cycles
instead he could recite
the names of all serpents
and he was the first to sight his brother
approach from the east
the tip of the feather on its head
the sun

for nothing i know of
i didn't tell them the pains were real
it is for the exact purpose
i sit here
now a victim of the earth's
rotating axis
the inherent seasons
outside
the snow is blowing violently
it seems to sit still but it meanders

covering and recovering
our frosted automobiles
the sun warms us through its tinted
filter and i think that when
we were created he or they
took special care of designing
our eyes
like the edge of a roof over a house
the skin has grown over yours
the long hair grows on my hair now
i even go farther as to claim
i must have been disillusioned
somehow turning the beautiful
to its limits
i went and now live where i wanted to go
all too suddenly i destroy things
which are in essence
ongoing like for instance time
when i first encountered the mute
at my doorstep who conveyed
he was my brother and proceeded to draw
a square into the air in front of him
with his two fingers entitled *assuage her*
it didn't matter
i had grown overanxious
and when i visualized the two animations
which were in between them
i relinquished that i had been correct
in not going out to the night
to go through the trouble of ritual
a ritual which should have ended before
and now our faces have reversed themselves
i see you walking into night
while i walk past you into day

for what holds me together now
it comes without the foam
from the ocean
it resembles a dream of a seagull-faced man
scurrying down the path of a wooded hill

bringing news of the man
a neighbor
who died from unnatural causes
there were bullets blessed and laden
with the odor of herbs
they momentarily appeared on his palms
he said take discretion
symbolic stones
watch me walk by somewhere
intoxicated
i thought it was a severe case
of an unwashed face
but when i observed closely
he had been stumbling from house to house
announcing the first day of his fast
right in the middle of summer
instead of the appropriate winter
in his decrepit face i saw the bounced
reflection of the sunlight someone had sent
from the underbrush with a mirror
his transience was clear

a woman who once made love
to the starblanket-wrapped man spoke
of clubbing gophers and foxes
basing her strength within the adoration
of them
she sat in its season
its backfire is the prisoner
she relates to a pair
of hands whose time
from abstention
found themselves behind iron bars
they were seen the winter previous
going their way reverently to the river
and on each occasion
they would have a new blanket
wrapped around the beaded
scabbard

she desires for someone to leave
cow innards for the owl outside
perhaps it's just hungry
it's probably why he comes
each night
the summer is gone anyway
the night is a stone wall with a mural
of our reenactment
and the smiling mask
over the train's face
whizzes by empty in mechanical grace

the worst possible has retreated
but now i worry over what to her is
life
in return and for the mutuality
of her existence
she is asked and she consents
unhampered by the below zero
weather
to cook for the temporal people
who sit all night singing rhymes
bilingually
to the two-faced haloed ram
all day their eyes are glazed
with the brown fluid of cactus
the little girl will remember her name
and the mournful singing of happy birthday
being flicked as ashes
from a cigarette of corn husk
that later her father would die
driving through the rain
to have thought one's self protected
in the very substance
which made you knowledgeable
living on its impediment
diversity
unique yes but i question why they are unable
to cook for themselves

there was a time she stopped walking
and a carved wooden face constructed
from elm   pine   cottonwood   hickory   oak
maple   and   sycamore
was directly aligned with her face
readjusting
her earrings she concluded its purpose
was aesthetic
except for the inconsistent noises
from the dishes in their racks
her sleep had been virtually unbothered
and she felt at ease until
she entered her father's room
moccasined feet trampled across the ceiling
where she had just been
all the drawers to his dresser were open
his personal effects were in disarray
next
she heard the scraping of a dog's claws
resisting the forceful shove from the doorway
onto the kitchen floor

demented indians from the city flocked
to the carrion they left
self-injected
they held mundane meetings
discussed at length the importance
of refrigerating their lunches
acquiring larger mugs for their coffee
to jobs they didn't want
they sent out mimeographed newsletters
in one the ability to type and compute
was a prerequisite for a one-day office-cleaning
job
caucasian wives straggled along
they were satisfied with toothless alcoholics
affairs with men their husbands
once treated

the lesbians downstairs are listening
to man-music
one of them imitates the man-singing
tomorrow
they'll receive the genitals of a wild pig
by mail
reason: they have no respect for peace
in the frames of my film
i scrutinize in detail the black-eared
pig and its markings

yesterday evening i heard the cry
of an eagle flying by
it's incongruous to think of the mouse
who sleeps under the seats of our nova ss
he has gone on drunks with us
subsisting on drops from our chins
of sloe gin
later he is the mouse
to turn against us
making his death imperative
my relatives would take word
of his action to a *visitor*
and i would be late
blanketless
in talking to him
to learn the consequences of his communion
with the animal

march eight/1979

for the eagles it is as it should be,
circling high above the settlement's ridge,
the three of them a family,
bonded permanently by the child
who hasn't yet seen us,
driving to him below on top
of grandmother universe,
avoiding the slushy potholes,
intent on filming them.

the father, russell;
the mother, joann;
their red-faced son, elgin, *ba ke ka maa qwi*,
fresh to this world, the air,
the skylight.

i pray for him that we shall one day
meet and talk in mutual good health
and i to explain to him my incredible joy,
how my mixed depression was momentarily
quelled.